American Red Cross

Together, we can save a life

babysitter's training Handbook

The following organizations provided expert review
of the *Babysitter's Training Handbook:*

BOYS & GIRLS CLUBS
OF AMERICA

BOY SCOUTS OF AMERICA

Girl Scouts.

jcc
association

StayWell

StayWell

Important certification information

Instructors authorized by the American Red Cross may issue American Red Cross certificates upon successful completion of a training program that uses this handbook as an integral part of the course. By itself, the text material does not constitute comprehensive Red Cross training. Only courses authorized by the Red Cross and taught by Red Cross authorized instructors are eligible for certification.

This handbook is an integral part of the American Red Cross Babysitter's Training program. It does not constitute complete and comprehensive training for first aid or CPR. Please contact your local Red Cross chapter for further first aid and CPR training.

The emergency care procedures outlined in this handbook reflect the standard of knowledge and accepted emergency practices in the United States at the time this book was published. It is the reader's responsibility to stay informed of changes in the emergency care procedures.

The Care Steps outlined within this product are consistent with the Guidelines 2000 for Emergency Cardiopulmonary Resuscitation and Emergency Cardiovascular Care.

Printed in the United States of America

Composition by Accu-color
Printing/binding by Banta

StayWell
780 Township Line Road
Yardley, PA 19067

ISBN 1-58480-138-7

06 / 9 8 7 6 5

ii

Acknowledgments

The Babysitter's Training program and this handbook were developed and produced through a joint effort of the American Red Cross and StayWell. Many individuals shared in the overall process in supportive, technical and creative ways. This course could not have been developed without the dedication of both employees and volunteers. Their commitment to excellence made this course and handbook possible.

The Babysitter's Training Development Team at American Red Cross national headquarters responsible for the design of this course and handbook included:

Tab Bates
Project Manager
Manager, Research and Product
Development

Casey M. Berg
Associate, Research and Product
Development

Martha Chapin
Customer Support Lead
Senior Associate, Customer Support
and Program Administration

Ted T. Crites, CHES
Senior Associate, Research and Product
Development

Eric Daniel
Business Planning & System Design Lead
Senior Associate, Business Planning &
System Design

Marc Madden
Technical Development Lead
Associate, Research and Product
Development

Darcy Olive
Associate, Research and Product
Development

Greta Petrilla
Marketing Lead
Manager, Communication and
Marketing

Shari Siuta
Evaluation Lead
Analyst, Research and Product
Development

Nicole Warden
Communications Lead
Associate, Office of the Vice President

The StayWell Editorial and Production Team included:

Nancy Monahan
Vice President

Paula Batt
Director of Sales

Reed Klanderud
Director of Marketing

Martha Sasser
Director of Editorial

Bill Winneberger
Director of Manufacturing

Shannon Bates
Senior Project Manager

Shawn Stout
Editorial Project Manager

Special thanks go to:

Ray Baquero-Cruz
Heartland Chapter

Dee Berry
Greater Cleveland Chapter
American Red Cross

Margie Fedders
Middletown, OH

Rochelle Gutierrez
American Red Cross Badger Chapter

Linda Olsen
Hollywood, FL

Kathleen Pepin
Omaha, NE

Susan Wooley, Ph.D., CHES
American School Health Association
Committee Member
American School Health
Association
Advisory Council on First Aid and
Safety (ACFAS)

Guidance and review were also provided by the following youth at the American
Red Cross:

Abby Coyne
Alexandria, VA

Morgan Chapin
Washington, DC

Taylor Dodson
Washington, DC

Jeremy McIntyre
Bordentown, NJ

External review was provided by the following organizations and individuals:

Rose Ann G. Soloway, RN, MSEd, DABAT
Associate Director, American
Association of Poison Control Centers
Clinical Toxicologist, National Capital
Poison Center

Barbara Taylor
YMCA of the USA
Chicago, IL

Elaine A. Tyrrell
Director, Outreach Programs
U.S. Consumer Product Safety
Commission
Washington, DC

Rachel C. Falgout
Assistant Director, Health and Life Skills
Boys & Girls Clubs of America
Atlanta, GA

Donna L. Nye
Membership, Program, and Diversity
Consultant
Girl Scouts of the U.S.A.
New York, NY

Bill Evans
Director, Outdoor Venturing
Boy Scouts of America
Irving, TX

Steven Becker
HPER Consultant
Jewish Community Centers Association
New York, NY

Kathleen Vos
4-H Curriculum Specialist
University of Wisconsin—Extension
Madison, WI

Those individuals supporting the Babysitter's Training project team included:

Pat Bonifer-Tiedt
Director, Research and Product
Development

LaKeva Lucas
Administrative Support, Research and
Product Development

Earl Harbert
Manager, Contract and Financial
Management

The following American Red Cross national headquarters employees provided additional guidance and review:

Steve Denne
Senior Director, Health and Safety
Services Operations

Susan Thurner
Manager, Research and Product
Development

Kathy Scruggs
Senior Associate, Southeast Region
Chapter Business Development & Sales
Support
Birmingham, AL

Rosa Villoch
Diversity Associate, Corporate Diversity
Department

The following American Red Cross national headquarters volunteer provided guidance and review:

Pamela Mack
Senior Associate, Volunteers, Youth
and Nursing

Special thanks go to the following individual for her assistance:

Kelly McCutcheon
Cover Design

CONTENTS

First Aid Action Plans 118

GETTiNG STARTED

Be Safe and Responsible

What makes a "good" babysitter who is asked back again and again? There is no one characteristic that makes someone a good babysitter. A good babysitter successfully uses leadership, basic care, safety and safe play and first aid. This course has been designed around these four major themes. Throughout the *American Red Cross Babysitter's Training Handbook*, we use four icons or symbols to remind you of the major themes of babysitting.

 The star represents leadership. A babysitter shows leadership when he or she ensures children's safety, encourages safe play, provides basic care and first aid and demonstrates professionalism.

 The heart represents basic care. A babysitter's basic care responsibilities include cleanliness and personal hygiene, feeding, diapering, toileting, rest, sleep, holding and dressing.

 The stop sign reminds you to stop and think about all of your actions when babysitting. Do your part to prevent accidents and illnesses by identifying solutions to safety-related problems.

 The bandage represents the first aid information. Using the emergency action steps: Check-Call-Care, babysitters can decide how to respond to an emergency.

Babysitters use the symbols of the star, heart, stop sign and bandage to remember qualities needed to have a successful babysitting business.

Babysitting Cast of Characters

By enrolling in the American Red Cross Babysitter's Training course, you are taking an important first step toward becoming a safe, responsible and successful babysitter. All the babysitter characters in this handbook represent safe, responsible and successful babysitters. Their job is to help you gain knowledge and skills to become a really great babysitter. You will see these characters throughout this Babysitter's Training Handbook, and they will guide you to become a skilled and confident babysitter.

How to Use the American Red Cross Babysitter's Training Handbook

This Babysitter's Training Handbook is to be used when taking the American Red Cross Babysitter's Training course. Your instructor will direct you to certain pages in this handbook. Go ahead and write on the Activity Pages for class activities. This is YOUR book.

You should continue using this handbook after the course and use it whenever you babysit. Look in the back of this book for First Aid Action Plans, starting on page 118. These plans explain how to take care of different kinds of injuries, emergencies and illnesses children can experience. The First Aid Action Plans are easy to find because of the orange border on the edges of the pages.

We have highlighted in red type those terms that you might need more information about and have explained them in the glossary at the back of this book.

Just for fun, this handbook also contains some games and puzzles. These activities will test your babysitting knowledge and skills. Try them out at home after class. You'll enjoy them and learn more, too!

Hi! I'm Redi, your babysitting mascot! I'll be with you through the whole book!

Getting Off to the Right Start in Babysitting

Before you begin your career as a professional babysitter, you should first discuss with your parents or guardians their overall expectations for you as a babysitter. Not every babysitting job will be right for you. Knowing what you can do and what you like to do, as well as your limitations, will help you find the right jobs. You should also rate how well you did after each babysitting job is over. Doing these things will help you have a safe, responsible and successful babysitting experience. They show that you take the responsibility of babysitting seriously—that you are a professional. You will also become a better babysitter over time.

Professional Behavior from Beginning to End

What does it mean to be professional? Babysitting is a job that requires a lot of responsibility. People who hire you trust you with the care of their children and their house. They are looking for a lot of things when they hire a babysitter.

First, they want someone who is mature and has the right skills to watch their children safely. They also want someone who is reliable. It doesn't matter if you are the best babysitter in the world—if you are late or cancel appointments all the time, you won't receive job offers. Parents or guardians also want someone who gets along with their children. Being professional means all this. Having a professional attitude will get you more babysitting jobs.

Good Business Practices

Good business practices are guidelines for the way you should act while on the job. For each job, you should:

◆ Discuss with your parents or guardians where and when you are asked to babysit before you accept the job. Also, let them know how many children you will be caring for, their ages and any special conditions about the job (for example, you will be preparing a simple meal; you will be taking the children to the playground, park or zoo; or you will be working with a child who has special needs).

◆ Make sure you are free to babysit and your family doesn't have anything scheduled.

◆ Remind them about the job before you go. Tell them when the job starts, how you will get to and from the job safely and when you'll be back home.

◆ Leave the name, address and telephone number of the family for whom you're babysitting with your parents.

◆ Discuss with your parents or guardians afterward anything unusual or disturbing that happened.

Remember, you should always follow these general good business practices:

◆ Always treat the family as your customer.

◆ Dress for the job in clean, comfortable clothes.

◆ Get to the job early or on time.

◆ Learn the house rules where you are babysitting before the job starts. (See the Family Interview Form, pages 13–17.)

◆ Treat the children and family with the same courtesy you expect for yourself.

◆ Report to the parents or guardians before you leave the job. (See the Babysitter's Report Record, pages 40–42.)

◆ Never talk about what you see or hear in the homes where you babysit (except with your parents, guardians or someone you trust).

◆ Discuss babysitting problems or concerns with someone you trust.

◆ Never look through belongings or rooms where you babysit unless the children's parents or guardians ask you to.

◆ Never cancel a babysitting job unless you have an emergency or are ill.

◆ Tell the parents or guardians as soon as you know you cannot babysit.

- Work to improve your babysitting skills by:
  - Taking additional courses at your local Red Cross chapter;
  - Reviewing this handbook to enhance your knowledge on topics such as leadership, prevention, basic care and first aid;
  - Keeping a diary of your experiences;
  - Practicing patience with children;
  - Creating fun activities to do with kids;
  - Reviewing your decisions made on the job;
  - Asking the kids you babysit for their feedback on your performance to help you fine tune your abilities (if they are old enough); and
  - Working with experienced babysitters.

I always work to improve my skills.

BABYSITTER'S SELF-ASSESSMENT TOOL

● ● ●

Answer these questions to discover your skills, abilities, likes and dislikes about babysitting. There are no right or wrong answers. Update the Babysitter's Self-Assessment Tool every 6 months.

Background and Experience

1 The number of babysitting jobs I have had is:

___ None.   ___ 1–3.   ___ 4–6.   ___ 7–10.   ___ More than 10.

2 The most children I have cared for at one time is:

___ 1.   ___ 2.   ___ 3.   ___ 4.   ___ 5 or more.

3 The youngest child I have ever cared for is a(n):

___ Infant (newborn to 12 months). ___ Preschooler (3 to 5 years).

___ Toddler (1 to 3 years).   ___ School-aged child (5 years and older).

4 The oldest child I have ever cared for is a(n):

___ Infant (newborn to 12 months). ___ Preschooler (3 to 5 years).

___ Toddler (1 to 3 years).   ___ School-aged child (5 years and older).

5 The longest babysitting job I ever had lasted:

___ 1 hour.   ___ 2–3 hours.   ___ 3–5 hours.   ___ 5–8 hours.

___ More than 8 hours.

6 I have accepted babysitting jobs (check all that apply):

___ On weekdays.   ___ In my neighborhood.

___ On weeknights.   ___ Outside my neighborhood.

___ On weekend days.   ___ On weekend nights.

___ During vacation times. ___ During the school year.

Special Skills and Abilities

7 My special abilities that make me a great babysitter are (check all that apply):

___ Music.   ___ Patience.   ___ Like kids.

___ Arts and crafts.   ___ Creativity.   ___ Sports.

___ Problem solving.   ___ Good student.   ___ Staying calm in

___ Storytelling.   ___ Other: _____ .   an emergency.

8 My leadership skills include (check all that apply):

___ Making good decisions.

___ Communicating well with children.

___ Recognizing and respecting differences among children and families.

___ Correcting misbehavior appropriately.

___ Recognizing and making considerations for the developmental stages of children at different ages.

9 My safety skills include (check all that apply):

___ Getting information before the job begins.

___ Knowing how to perform infant and child CPR.

___ Knowing first aid.

___ Recognizing and removing or limiting safety-related problems.

___ Supervising children at all times.

___ Choosing appropriate play for children at different ages.

___ Keeping my Babysitter's Training Safety and First Aid Kit out of the children's reach.

___ Being a role model for safety.

___ Using the Safety Inspection Checklist, page 91.

10 My basic care skills include (check all that apply):

___ Following the family's instructions.

___ Washing my hands and helping children wash their hands.

___ Diapering children and helping them use the toilet.

___ Feeding children with a bottle or a spoon.

___ Helping children get rest and sleep.

___ Picking up children correctly.

___ Holding children correctly.

___ Giving appropriate care for children at different ages.

11 My first aid skills include (check all that apply):

___ Recognizing and acting promptly in an emergency.

___ Giving appropriate care for children at different ages.

___ Being certified in American Red Cross Infant & Child CPR and First Aid Basics.

Preferences

12 I prefer to care for (check all that apply):

___ One child at a time.

___ Several children at a time.

___ Infants.

___ Toddlers.

___ Preschoolers.

___ School-aged children.

13 The time of day I can babysit is:

___ Mornings.   ___ Afternoons.

___ Evenings.   ___ Nights.

14 I prefer to get rides to and from jobs:

___ From my parents.

___ From the children's parents or guardians.

___ On my own.

15 I absolutely do NOT want to babysit when _____

_____.

Parent Assessment

Instructions
Ask your parents or guardians these questions. Be sure they approve and support your babysitting plans.

16 My parents or guardians will (check all that apply):

____ Take me to and from jobs.

____ Be available by phone when I am on the job.

____ Tell me which jobs they will not allow me to accept.

____ Tell me their rules for my babysitting jobs.

____ Work with me to make sure that my Babysitter's Training Safety and First Aid Kit is fully supplied for each babysitting job.

17 My parents or guardians will not allow me to accept these jobs:

_____

_____

_____

_____

_____

18 My parents' or guardians' rules for my babysitting jobs are:

_____

_____

_____

_____

_____

19 My parents or guardians will let me know on
_____(date) if I can babysit.

BLANK RÉSUMÉ

● ● ●

Use the blank résumé on the next page to help you apply for babysitting jobs. Fill in the blanks to create your résumé. Then you can print or type your résumé on a clean sheet of paper to give to parents who may want to hire you. Use the space below to draw what you would like your résumé to look like.

RÉSUMÉ

● ● ●

Name: _____

Address: _____

Phone: _____

E-mail Address: _____

Education: Your School _____

             Your Grade _____

Training: American Red Cross Babysitter's Training course

             Helping children behave, basic care, safety and safe play, leadership and professionalism

Additional Training:

(Include whatever applies, such as an American Red Cross Infant & Child CPR or first aid course.)

Babysitting Experience:

Hobbies:

Skills and Abilities (from my Babysitter's Self-Assessment):

References: (List here the names and phone numbers of people you babysat for in the past year who say it is okay to use them as references.)

Interviewing the Parents or Guardians and Assessing the Job

Before taking a babysitting job, always interview the family first. Not all babysitting jobs are the same. Some are harder than others. Meet the children and find out as much as you can about the job during your interview with the parents or guardians. Ask about:

☐ *Transportation*. How are you going to get to and from the job safely?

☐ *Number of children*. Care for only as many children as you are sure you can handle safely. For most babysitters, that means no more than three children. For more than three children, you will need help. Ask if you can bring along a friend to help; your friend should also be paid. If you decide to bring a friend, make sure he or she is involved in the interview process. Notify the parents that you may need to bring a helper and arrange a meeting time.

☐ *Ages of children*. Younger children usually need more care. Infants need a lot of care. Toddlers are always on the go. Preschoolers and school-aged children need your full attention, too. Do not take jobs where you are expected to watch several young children by yourself.

☐ *Length of time*. Long hours make the job harder. While you are new to babysitting, you may want to limit your jobs to 2 or 3 hours.

☐ *Time of day*. Watching children at night while they sleep is usually easier than watching them during the day.

☐ *Responsibilities*. Don't say you will do other chores like cooking or bathing a child unless you have been trained to do so. Your first responsibility is to keep yourself and the children safe.

☐ *House rules*. Know the house rules for both yourself and the children.

☐ *Children with special needs*. You might be a babysitter for a child with special emotional, physical or learning needs or a child who is hard to control. Some children need special equipment like a wheelchair. Agree to babysit for children with special needs only if the parents or guardians train you in the specific areas of special things you will need to do and you feel comfortable with the tasks and responsibilities. Make sure your parents or guardians are aware that you're taking care of a child with special needs.

Interviewing Tips

The Family Interview Form on pages 13–17 lists questions to ask. Make copies of the Family Interview Form and take one with you the first time you meet with a family. Be sure to look over the form BEFORE you get there so that you remember what's on it. Don't just hand it to the parents or guardians to fill out. It's better to politely ask the questions yourself so that you can find out about any problems or special things that might come up. Also, fill out the Family Information Cards in the back of the book for a quick reference to emergency numbers and information.

Feel free to ask a lot of questions to make sure you find out everything you need to know to do a good job. Relax and be friendly. Tell the parents or guardians about yourself: how old you are, where you go to school, why you want the job and what you like best about babysitting. Then you can start asking questions about the family. Ask the family to include the children in the interview as well (meeting the children during the interview will help when you come back to babysit).

The interview is your chance to make sure the job is right for you. You'll also find out everything you need to know to be a GREAT babysitter for the family—the kind of babysitter the children love to be with and who gets asked back again and again! While you are interviewing the family to see if you want to babysit for them, they are also interviewing you. This way, everyone can decide if you and the job are the right match. Remember, you are the one who has to decide if you want this job; you can say no if it is not right for you.

FAMiLY iNTERViEW FORM
● ● ●

Family Information and Emergency Numbers	
Family name:	**Child's name Age Weight:**
Phone number:	1. _____
Address:	
E-mail address:	2. _____
Nearest cross-street:	3. _____

Phone number where parent or guardian can be reached:	Local emergency phone number:
Cellular phone number:	Doctor's name:
Pager number:	Doctor's phone number:
Neighbor's name and phone number:	Poison Control Center (PCC): (800) 222-1222

Household Rules and Discipline

What are the household rules? How would you like me to handle misbehavior?	
Do the children need to complete any homework or chores? Would you like me to make sure that these are done?	

Safety and Play

Would you take me on a tour of your house? I would like to go over the Babysitter's Safety Inspection Checklist with you.	
Does your family have a fire escape plan? If not, can you have one in place before I begin?	
Do your children know Stop, Drop and Roll?	

Does your house have working smoke alarms?	
Should I apply insect repellant or sunscreen lotion to the children when they play outside?	
Do you have any pets that I need to care for? Are they friendly to strangers?	
May I meet your children and pets before I babysit?	
What are your family's rules for play? What are your children's favorite play activities?	
Are there any play areas or activities that are off-limits or restricted?	
How do I work the door and window locks?	
Is there a spare house key for me to use?	

Basic Care

How do you want me to handle handwashing and brushing and flossing teeth?	
What can your children eat and drink? Will I be preparing any simple meals? Do your children have any food allergies?	
What are the routines for diapering and using the toilet? Where are the supplies of baby wipes and cleaning materials kept? Where do you want me to put dirty diapers and soiled disposable gloves?	

What are the routines for quiet time, bedtime and naps? When is bedtime? Do your children have a favorite bedtime story? Do they like a light on? Do you prefer their door open or closed?	
What do you want your children to wear for outdoor play? For naptime? For bedtime?	
Where do I put dirty clothing?	
Is there any equipment I might be using to take care of the children that you want to show me?	
Are there any medical conditions or medications that I should be aware of? If the child is taking medication, where is it kept? Would you please fill out this Parental Consent and Contact Form (see pages 18–19 or go to www.redcross.org to download the form) in case something happens? What do I need to know?	
Where is your first aid kit kept?	
Where is your disaster supply kit kept?	
Are there any special care needs for your children? Tutoring? Music practice? Sports practice? Faith practices?	
Are there any special care needs for your pets?	
Is there anything else I need to be aware of?	

Business Basics

What is the date and beginning and ending time of the job?	
Should I answer the phone? If so, how should I answer it?	
Are there any rules I should observe in your home? May I use the TV, radio or computer? May I make a short personal call? Am I allowed to do homework? May I fix a snack?	
I usually charge $_____ for my hourly rate. Is that okay with you?	

PARENTAL CONSENT AND CONTACT FORM

● ● ●

This form is to be completed and signed by the child's parent or legal guardian. The signature of the parent or legal guardian indicates permission for the babysitter to follow and act in accordance with these instructions.

Name of Child: _____

Date of Birth: _____

Medical Condition(s) of Concern:

_____

_____

_____

Signs and/or Symptom(s) to Watch for:

_____

_____

List the Child's Medications, Prescription and Over-the-Counter:

Medication: _____   Dose: _____

How Given: _____   When Given: _____

Special Instructions (to be taken with, etc.): _____

Possible Side Effects: _____

Medication: _____   Dose: _____

How Given: _____   When Given: _____

Special Instructions (to be taken with, etc.): _____

Possible Side Effects: _____

Medication: _____ Dose: _____

How Given: _____ When Given: _____

Special Instructions (to be taken with, etc.): _____

Possible Side Effects: _____

*I give permission for _____
("Babysitter") to administer medicine(s) to the child named above in
the manner described above.*

*Further, I give my permission to the Babysitter to provide basic first
aid for the child named above and to take the appropriate measures
including contacting the emergency medical services (EMS) system
and arranging for transportation to _____
_____ or the nearest medical facility to
receive the appropriate level of care as determined by qualified medical professionals.*

*In the event the child named above is injured or ill, I understand that
the Babysitter will attempt to contact me, the other parent or legal
guardian at the contact numbers listed below.*

Parent/Legal Guardian's Name: _____

Contact Numbers _____ on _____ (hours/days)

_____ on _____ (hours/days)

_____ on _____ (hours/days)

_____   _____

Parent/Legal Guardian Signature   Date

Telephone Safety Tips

Always:

◆ Ask the parents or guardians how or if they would like the phone answered.

◆ Be polite and brief when answering the phone.

◆ Write down the message, as well as the caller's name, the time of the call and the caller's phone number.

◆ Use the phone for calls related to the job only, not for personal calls, unless the parents have given you permission to use it for a short personal call (i.e., you need a homework question from a friend). Remember, you may tie up the phone line when you use the Internet. Get the parents' permission to use the Internet.

◆ Call the parents or guardians, an adult you trust or the police if you get a call that scares you.

◆ Make sure emergency phone numbers are posted by all phones.

◆ Make sure the address of where you are babysitting is posted by all phones.

Never:

◆ Leave the children alone while answering the phone.

◆ Tell callers that you are the babysitter or that the parents or guardians are away. Instead, say, "Mr. or Mrs. _____ is busy right now. May I take a message?"

EMERGENCY NUMBERS
9-1-1
POISON CONTROL CENTER
(800) 222-1222

◆ Call your friends or have them call you for a long conversation while on the job. You could miss an important call from the children's parents or guardians or you may not hear the children if they call to you or become ill.

20

Personal Safety Tips

Your own health and safety are just as important as the health and safety of the children you babysit.

◆ Get to know the parents or guardians and the families of the children you will babysit.

◆ Tell your parents or guardians where you will be, when to expect you home and how to contact you. Know where they will be and how to contact them.

◆ If babysitting for a family makes you feel uncomfortable, don't babysit for them.

◆ Make your own arrangements to get to and from the job safely. Have a back-up plan ready. (Example: If you are uncomfortable riding home with a parent or guardian, have a code word that you can use on the telephone to let your parents or guardians know that you need a ride home.)

◆ Don't wear jewelry that dangles or has sharp edges. It can scratch or hurt you or the children.

◆ Keep your clothing neat and your hair out of the way so they do not get caught in anything.

◆ Keep your fingernails short and your hands clean to prevent the spread of **germs**.

◆ Don't babysit when you are sick.

◆ Don't use alcohol, tobacco or other drugs.

◆ Keep your first aid kit handy but out of the children's reach.

◆ Know and respect your limits. Don't take a job or try to do something you're not sure about.

◆ Take your Babysitter's Training Handbook with you and use it as a reference while on the job.

I always have my Handbook when I babysit!

Tips for Preventing Emergencies Inside and Outside of the Home

In the Home

Never:

◆ Open the door to anyone, including the parents or guardians, before checking to see who is there. Look out through a peep-hole or window first.

◆ Open the door to strangers.

◆ Open the door to delivery people. Ask them to leave the package at the door or tell them to come back another time.

◆ Let anyone inside who is using alcohol or drugs, even if you know them.

◆ Have your friends over to visit while you are babysitting unless discussed prior in the Family Interview Form on pages 13–17.

◆ Stay in a situation where you or the children are being threatened by a parent, guardian or anyone else. Immediately take the children to a safe place. A safe place could be a neighbor's home; a school; a church, mosque or synagogue; a local business; or a police or fire station.

◆ Stay anywhere that you smell smoke or hear a fire or smoke alarm. Get the children and yourself outside. Ask a neighbor to call the fire department.

Outside the Home

Never:

◆ Talk to strangers. If someone keeps trying to talk to you, ignore them and take the children to a safe area.

◆ Go outside to check out an unusual noise. If you are worried about it, call the parents or guardians, an adult you trust or the police.

Special Concerns

Child abuse is the term for hurting a child physically, emotionally or sexually. Some children who are abused are not fed, washed or clothed properly. Some indications of child abuse include:

◆ An abused child may have bruises, burns or scars. Often, physically abused children are afraid of contact, such as hugging or being held.

◆ An abused child may have low self-esteem, seem very sad or cry a lot, act quiet or be very loud and aggressive.

◆ A sexually abused child may be afraid to undress or have physical contact with anyone. He or she may have signs of physical abuse.

If you think a child in your care has been abused, don't ask the child about it. Tell an adult you trust, like your parent or guardian or a teacher, about your concerns and ask him or her for help. Your actions can be important to protect the child. If the first adult tells you to ignore the situation, tell another. Call the police if you are unsure or feel the situation is life threatening.

SELF-EVALUATION AFTER THE JOB

● ● ●

Things I need to think about after I finish a babysitting job:

◆ How well did I do on this job?

◆ What went well?

◆ What happened that I was afraid I couldn't handle?

◆ What should I do differently next time?

◆ Could I have better prepared myself for this job? How?

◆ Will I babysit for this family again? If not, why not?

◆ How well did I use my babysitting records and reports?

◆ Other comments:

LEADERSHIP: SAFE AND RESPONSIBLE BABYSITTING

● ● ●

The Babysitter as a Leader and Role Model

Parents and guardians rely on you to keep their children safe while they are away. You are a leader because children look to you as the responsible person in charge. A leader makes thoughtful decisions and knows how to use his or her skills.

You are also a role model for the children in your care. Young children watch what you do and how you handle yourself in different situations. They are likely to act in the same way you do.

As a babysitter, you can be a good leader and role model by:

◆ Keeping yourself and the children safe;

◆ Communicating well with both the children and the parents or guardians;

◆ Making decisions carefully;

◆ Guiding the children's behavior appropriately;

◆ Respecting the diversity of people and households;

◆ Using tools that can help you do a better job, such as the Babysitter's Training Handbook and the Babysitter's Training Safety and First Aid Kit; and

◆ Evaluating yourself after each job and making improvement as needed.

Respecting House Rules

Before accepting a babysitting job, use the Family Interview Form, pages 13–17, to learn as much as you can from the parents or guardians about their children and about house rules. The parents or guardians can tell you what to expect and how they handle certain situations. The children will be happier and will feel more secure if you follow their usual routines. This is especially comforting for children who become upset when their parents or guardians are away from home.

Reporting to the Parents or Guardians

When the parents or guardians return home, take a few minutes to tell them how things went. Use the Babysitter's Report Record, pages 40–42.

Follow these guidelines:

◆ *Be positive.* Tell them good things about their children.

◆ *Be specific.* Tell them exactly what happened and be sure to report if anything out of the ordinary occurred.

◆ *Be complete.* Report anything unusual that happened (i.e., a young child who usually goes to sleep easily cried when getting ready for bed).

◆ *Be honest.* Tell them if a child misbehaved or if you had a problem with anything.

◆ *Be polite.* Treat the parents or guardians with courtesy and respect.

Respecting Diversity

People are alike in many ways. In other ways, people are very different. These differences are called diversity. Diversity is a good thing. Without diversity, everyone would be exactly the same and that would make the world a very boring place. Accept each infant or child as someone special. You may find that the infants or children you babysit are diverse in some of the following ways:

◆ *Age and development.* Children change as they get older. An older child does not play the same as an infant because of differences in development.

> **How can I do the best job?**

26

- *Developmental stages.* **Developmental stages** describe how typical infants and children grow and what they can do at certain ages. The developmental stages described later in this lesson are guidelines, not rules. Many infants and children act in different ways even at the same ages and stages. Refer to pages 32—33 to help you decide on appropriate and safe play and basic care.

- *Gender.* Boys and girls may act the same way and do the same things even though they are physically different. Both boys and girls may enjoy sports, reading, playing games and watching television.

- *Individual differences.* Infants and children can vary in their responses to the same situation. Some infants or children do not seem to be bothered by anything, while others cry very easily.

- *Cultural differences.* If you babysit for an infant or child whose family is from a different country or culture than your own, the family might speak with an accent, look or dress differently than you. They might have different customs and ways of doing things. You can learn a lot from these families — all about new foods, customs and holidays. This is also a fun way to learn new words. Respect all of these differences.

- *Religious beliefs.* You may care for children with religious beliefs different from your own. The parents might give special instructions, such as "Make sure Johnnie says his prayers" or "Make sure Suzy doesn't eat meat." Respect each family's religion.

- *Family members.* You might care for infants or children living with one parent, with a stepparent or guardian or with other relatives who are not the infant or child's parents. Respect all family members.

- *Special needs children.* You may care for children who have special needs. Be patient with them; their bodies and minds may work differently than yours.

- *Family income.* All families do not have the same amount of money to spend. Infants and children have different kinds of toys and clothes. Give the same good care to all infants and children, no matter how much the family spends on clothes, toys, food and other things.

Making Decisions

In many problem situations, you will know what to do if you follow the guidelines in this handbook. For example, if an infant or child has a cut that needs bandaging, follow the first aid steps in the First Aid Action Plans. In other situations, you'll have to make decisions on your own, such as what to do when an infant or child is misbehaving. In these situations, use the FIND Decision-Making Model to help you decide what to do.

FIND Decision-Making Model

Step 1: Figure out the problem.

◆ What do you have to decide?

◆ Focus on the exact problem that is causing trouble.

Step 2: Identify solutions.

◆ What are your choices?

◆ Think about all possible ways you could solve the problem.

Step 3: Name the positive and negative consequences of each choice.

◆ Think about the positive and negative consequences of each way to solve the problem.

Step 4: Decide which is the best choice, then act on it.

◆ Decide which is the best solution.

Use the FIND model to help make the best possible decision!

FIND DECISION-MAKING MODEL ACTIVITY

• • •

Your instructor will tell you how to fill out the next page during class.

Figure

out the problem. "What do I need to decide?"

Identify

solutions. "What are my choices of what to do?"

Name

the positive and negative consequences of each choice. "What are the positive and negative consequences of each way to solve the problem?"

Decide

which is the best choice, then act on it. "What will I do now?"

FIND DECISION-MAKING MODEL ACTIVITY PAGE

I am confident with my decision!

F

i

N

D

Use the FIND model to help make the best possible decision!

Common Babysitting Problems: Using the FIND Decision-Making Model to Decide What to Do

Babysitters often encounter specific kinds of problems with children in their care, especially problems involving meals, homework or chores, TV or video games and bedtime. Below are common babysitting problems with some possible solutions. Think about which solutions would work best for you and why. What are some other solutions you could use while on the job? Practice using the FIND Decision-Making Model to decide what to do.

Problem: Child refuses to eat dinner.

Some possible FIND solutions:

◆ If you can, give the child choices, such as carrots or green beans, macaroni and cheese or spaghetti.

◆ If the child becomes hungry later on, offer the dinner he or she first refused.

◆ Explain to the child that if he or she won't eat dinner, he or she will not get any dessert or snacks for the rest of the evening.

Problem: Child refuses to pick up toys.

Some possible FIND solutions:

◆ Don't let the child get out new toys until the other toys are put away.

◆ Offer to help the child put away the toys.

◆ Make clean-up fun. Suggest that the child put toys away by color; start with the child's favorite color.

AGES AND STAGES

● ● ●

Infant *(Newborn to 12 Months)*

◆ Reaches for objects

◆ Lifts chest off ground, supported by arms

◆ Smiles and laughs

◆ Rolls over

◆ Picks up and holds small objects

◆ Explores by putting things in mouth

◆ Supports own head (at about 6 months old)

◆ "Talks" baby talk or babbles (ma-ma, ba-ba, da-da, na-na)

◆ Crawls

◆ Acts shy with new people

◆ Gets into a sitting position (at about 6 to 8 months old)

◆ Waves and plays games like peeka-boo

◆ Pulls self up to a standing position (at about 9 to 12 months old)

◆ Stands alone for a second or two (at about 10 to 12 months old)

◆ Moves around by holding on to furniture for support: "cruising" (at about 9 to 12 months old)

◆ Claps hands

◆ Begins to take first steps

Toddler *(1 to 3 Years)*

◆ Drinks from a cup

◆ Walks well (younger toddler); runs well (older toddler)

◆ Feeds self (with hands first and then with small spoon and fork)

◆ Starts potty training (success may vary)

◆ Learns to talk (from single words to simple sentences; using over 50 words by age 2)

◆ Becomes easily frustrated

◆ Is physically active and busy

◆ Walks up steps, but needs help to be safe on steps (by about 19 months)

◆ Walks down steps, but needs help to be safe on steps (by about 2 years old)

◆ Builds with blocks

◆ Imitates simple adult activities (such as using a hairbrush or trying to open the door with keys)

◆ Brushes teeth (usually needs help until about 2 1/2 years old)

◆ Dresses self (with lots of supervision and help)

◆ Washes and dries hands (if able to reach the sink safely)

◆ Recognizes and names favorite people and objects

Preschooler
(3 to 5 Years)

- Balances on one foot, hops (tries to roller-skate by age 5)
- Moves constantly (can climb fences by age 5)
- Catches bouncing ball (can throw a ball overhand by age 4)
- Rides a tricycle (can ride bike with training wheels by age 4)
- Uses hands more (older child can do simple puzzles)
- Presses buttons on phone keypad
- Takes off shoes, socks and pants; puts on simple clothes (can dress, lace shoes and undress with supervision by age 4)
- Has more control of own toilet routine (may wear diaper or training pants at night)
- Washes hands and face (can do normal daily hygiene by age 5, but a little clumsy)
- Talks well and asks a lot of questions; memory improving

Infants and children are individuals. Many infants and children act in different ways, even if they are at the same ages and development stages!

School-Aged Child
(5 Years and Older)

- Arms and legs growing and becoming more coordinated (enjoys playing sports, jumping rope and skipping games by age 6 to 7)
- Weight and height increasing (faster for boys up to 9 years old)
- Dresses, bathes and eats by self with supervision
- Loses baby teeth; permanent teeth coming in
- Begins to follow rules and enjoys games with rules
- Tells difference between real and make-believe (begins to think out problems by age 7)
- Uses tools (paintbrushes or rulers)
- Uses electronic devices such as computers, TVs and radios on a regular basis
- Makes first attempts at learning to play music
- Learns to tell time
- Becomes more independent and self-reliant
- May enjoy collecting things as a hobby (by age 8)

Problem: Child refuses to go to bed.

Some possible FIND solutions:

◆ Prepare the child for bed ahead of time by saying it's time for bed right after the present activity is over.

◆ Make bedtime pleasant by reading the child a story or playing soft music.

◆ If the child still refuses to go to bed, say you will have to report this to the parents or guardians.

Problem: Child refuses to do homework.

Some possible FIND solutions:

◆ Don't let the child talk on the phone, watch television or do anything else until the homework is complete.

◆ Ask the child what he or she is studying in school. Ask to see the homework. Then guide him or her into doing the homework one step at a time. Show your interest and praise the child for doing the homework.

Problem: Infant will not stop crying.

Some possible FIND solutions:

◆ Pick up the infant and hold and comfort him or her.

◆ Burp the infant.

◆ Offer a bottle and see if the infant will take it.

◆ Check to see if the infant needs to have his or her diaper changed.

◆ Check to see if the infant's clothing is tight or uncomfortable.

Being a Good Communicator with Children

Knowing how to talk to and how to listen to children will make you a good communicator.

Keep It Simple
◆ Use short sentences and simple words to avoid confusing children.

Keep It Positive
◆ Tell children what you want them to do. For example, say, "Please put your plate in the sink" instead of, "Don't leave your plate on the table."

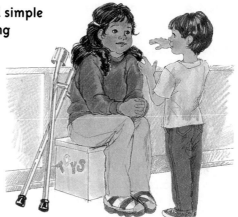

Be Specific
◆ Tell children exactly what you like or don't like about what they are doing. For example, say, "I like it when you pick up your toys," rather than, "You're a good girl."

Show Courtesy and Respect
◆ Say "please" and "thank you." Children will copy this behavior.

◆ Don't call children names. Name-calling makes children angry and causes hurt feelings. Calling children "stupid" or "bad" does not explain to them what they did wrong.

Stay Calm
◆ Talk in a calm voice when **disciplining** even if you are upset or angry. If a child screams or carries on, say, "I can't understand you when you yell."

Show You Are Listening
◆ If you can't do what the child wants right away, let the child know that you are listening and have heard his or her request. For example, if a child wants to go to the park and you need to ask his or her parent first, explain this to him or her. Children will not feel ignored if you show them you are listening.

Helping Children Behave

Children often need help learning how to control their behavior and how to express themselves. When a child is misbehaving, you can use different ways to encourage the child to stop or change the misbehavior.

When a child misbehaves, you have three choices of how you can take action:

◆ Do nothing.

◆ Say something.

◆ Physically do something.

Each of these methods works best in different situations.

◆ Doing nothing means you ignore the child's misbehavior. Doing nothing is a method you can use when a child is misbehaving to get your attention. Example: If a child throws a temper tantrum but is not hurting himself or herself or anyone else, you can ignore the behavior.

◆ Saying something means you tell the child what to do or what not to do. Saying something is a method you will use to solve most common babysitting problems. Example: A child is throwing a baseball against a wall in the house. You explain that playing catch with a baseball is an outside game. Then give the child a choice of playing with something else inside or taking the baseball outside.

◆ Physically doing something means you physically stop the child from misbehaving. Physically stop the child when the child's behavior is a physical threat to himself or herself or to others. Examples: If the child tries to hit you, grasp the child's arm before he or she can hit you and say, "I won't let you hit me. If you're angry, tell me with words." If the child is about to throw a toy, take the toy away.

Correcting the Behavior Without Criticizing the Child

Children need to know that you won't stop liking them if they misbehave. Make sure children know that you are unhappy with what they did, rather than with them. You can use positive feedback to help guide the behavior of children before they misbehave and give corrective feedback to give positive and respectful requests to stop or change their misbehavior. Babysitters should never shake, slap, spank, lock-up, shout at or make fun of children.

NEVER SHAKE A BABY OR A CHILD!

Shaking a baby or child in a moment of frustration or anger can cause serious harm or death. Babies have weak neck muscles and heavy heads, and when a baby is shaken, the head flops back and forth, causing serious damage. Shaking a baby or child can cause severe injury, resulting in problems ranging from brain damage to death.

Remember, no matter how frustrated or angry you feel — never shake a baby or child!

GOLD MEDAL PERFORMANCE CHECK-OFF

● ● ●

Your instructor will tell you how to fill out this page during class.

FIND Decision-Making Model
Did the babysitter:

☐   Figure out exactly what the problem was?

☐   Identify choices for possible solutions?

☐   Name the positive and negative consequences of each choice?

☐   Decide on the best solution?

Communication Skills of Babysitter
Did the babysitter use statements that were:

☐   Simple and clear?

☐   Positive?

☐   Specific?

☐   Courteous and respectful?

Did the babysitter:

☐ Use a calm voice?

☐ Acknowledge the child's feelings?

☐ Listen and respond to the child?

Helping Children Behave
Did the babysitter:

☐ Explain limits and rules?

☐ Consider the child's developmental stage?

☐ Give positive feedback?

☐ Use corrective feedback for undesired behavior?

☐ Correct misbehavior appropriately by doing nothing, saying something or physically doing something?

☐ Correct misbehavior in a positive way?

BABYSITTER'S REPORT RECORD
● ● ●

1. Household Rules and Discipline

a. I noticed these good behaviors:

_____

b. I used the discipline technique you asked me to use when:

_____

2. Safety

a. We received the following phone calls and visitors:

Date/time	Name	Reason for calling or visiting	Phone number to reach the caller or visitor

b. The following accidents and illnesses happened while you were gone:

Date/time	What happened	What I did	What the child did

3. Play

a. We played with the following games and toys:

_____

b. I noticed these good behaviors while we were playing:

_____

_____

4. Basic Care

a. We ate the following foods:

_____

b. _____ had naptime/went to bed at_____.

_____had naptime/went to bed at_____.

c. For _____ I changed the diaper/helped with toileting _____ times and I noticed _____

_____.

For _____ I changed the diaper/helped with toileting _____ times and I noticed _____

_____.

5. Other Comments

_____

_____

_____

_____

I gave _____ (child's name) the following medications and amounts exactly as instructed by

_____ (parent or guardian):

Time: _____Medicine: _____

Amount Given:_____

Any Reactions: _____

I provided the following first aid care for

_____(child's name).

What happened: _____

Where was the injury: _____

When did it happen: _____

What the child reported: _____

What I did: _____

SHINING STAR GAME
● ● ●

Instructions

Unscramble the words on leadership and professionalism to fill up the briefcase. Use the sample scramble to help you get started.

Sample

Before accepting a babysitting job, use the [ymafli tinwvieer] Form to learn as much as you can from the parents or guardians about their children and their house rules. (Answer: Family Interview)

1 You are a leader because children look to you as the [nispslerebo] person in charge.

_____

2 A good leader and role model [muntccaiesom] well with both the children and their parents or guardians.

_____

3 Part of having a [ssfproealion] attitude is being reliable.

_____

4 Good [sseusbin cctiespar] are guidelines for the way you should act while on the job.

_____

Answers are found on page 159!

BASIC CARE:
THE HEART OF BABYSITTING
● ● ●

An Overview of Basic Care

Basic care is the heart of babysitting. Effective basic care begins with understanding the family's routines for care. Routines, supplies and equipment can be different among families, so it is always important to ask parents or guardians about basic care preferences. Babysitters should model good basic care behaviors in their own activities. For example, you should concentrate on eating when it is mealtime, wash your hands before and after eating and after toileting, and get proper rest.

The Basics of Basic Care

◆ Safety;

◆ Cleanliness and personal hygiene;

◆ Holding;

◆ Feeding;

◆ Diapering and toileting;

◆ Dressing;

◆ Sleeping and resting; and

◆ Supervision.

I know all the basics!

Be a Good Role Model

◆ Wash your hands before and after assisting with toileting and handling food.

◆ Serve healthy snack foods.

◆ Choose calming activities for quiet times.

◆ Make sure children get enough rest.

◆ Supervise children while providing basic care.

Talking to the Parents or Guardians About Basic Care

Gather information about basic care that you will need to know before you babysit. See the Family Interview Form, pages 13–17.

◆ You will need to know what kinds of basic care skills you will use to care for the children.

◆ Children are usually happier if you stick to their basic care routines.

Report to the parents or guardians on basic care when you finish the job. Use the Babysitter's Report Record on pages 40–42.

Find out where basic care supplies are kept. This makes the job easier.

WATCH OUT FOR GERMS

● ● ●

While on the job, you could come in contact with germs. Germs can be transmitted by:

◆ Direct contact (such as getting blood, vomit or urine in a cut on your hand);

◆ Air (when breathing in droplets from someone else's cough or sneeze);

◆ Contact with an object or surface that has been in contact with a germ (such as a telephone receiver or fork and knife); and

◆ An insect, animal or human bite.

Some germs can cause you to get a cold or the flu or expose you to common childhood diseases like chicken pox and the measles. Other germs can cause serious diseases like HIV, the virus that causes AIDS.

To stay healthy and avoid the spread of germs, wash your hands often and wear disposable gloves if you could come into contact with blood or other body fluids. Many families may not have disposable gloves, so make sure you take some with you. The Babysitter's Training Safety and First Aid Kit contains disposable gloves, and you can also buy them at many supermarkets and drugstores. Be sure to find out in advance whether any children you will be caring for are allergic to latex. Many disposable gloves are made from latex, but there are also gloves made of vinyl or nitrile.

Use a new pair of disposable gloves:

◆ When you change a diaper;

◆ When you give first aid to someone who is bleeding; and

◆ When you touch any body fluids, such as urine, nasal discharge or vomit, or solid wastes like feces.

As a babysitter, you can become infected by serious diseases from coming into contact with blood, urine, feces or vomit without using gloves. Be sure to carefully remove and properly dispose of gloves after giving basic care. When you remove gloves, be careful that you do not get any body fluids on yourself. Wash your hands before providing care and after disposing of your gloves when you have completed basic care (see page 62 for how to remove gloves).

46 ♥

HANDWASHING

● ● ●

Handwashing is the best way to prevent passing germs and spreading infectious diseases.

Always wash your hands:

◆ Before you touch children;

◆ Before and after you prepare food;

◆ Before and after you eat;

◆ Before and after changing diapers or helping a child with toileting;

◆ After using the toilet;

◆ After playing outdoors;

◆ After touching insects, plants or pets;

◆ After cleaning up spills;

◆ Before and after giving first aid; and

◆ After coughing, sneezing or blowing your nose.

Make sure children wash their hands:

◆ Before and after they eat;

◆ After they use the toilet (wash the infant's hands after he or she is diapered, if dirty);

◆ After they touch objects or surfaces used by other people in public areas (e.g., after they come home from the playground);

◆ Before they put their hands in their mouths or touch their faces;

◆ After they cough, sneeze or blow their noses; and

◆ After they touch or handle insects, plants or pets.

PRACTICING HANDWASHING SKILLS
● ● ●

1 Remove watches and jewelry.

2 Wash for at least 20 seconds. Use soap (preferably a liquid soap) and warm running water. Scrub nails by rubbing them against the palms of your hands.

3 Rinse thoroughly.

5 Turn off the faucet using the paper towel. Throw the paper towel away.

I even wash my paws!

4 Dry your hands with a paper towel.

6 Put your watch and jewelry back on.

PICKING UP AND HOLDING CHILDREN
● ● ●

Most children enjoy being held, although some do not. Respect individual differences.

Picking Up and Holding Infants

◆ Slide both of your hands under the infant's underarms and wrap your fingers around the infant's ribs and support his or her head.

OR

◆ Slide one hand under the infant's head and back. Slide your other hand under the infant's bottom.

◆ Always support the head, neck and back of infants under 6 months old.

◆ Holding the infant close to your body makes the infant feel safe and secure.

Cradle Hold

1 Support the infant's bottom and lower back with one hand.

2 Cradle the infant in your arm and support the back with your other arm. Hold the infant's head near or at the bend of the elbow.

3

Hold the infant close to your body, with the infant's back straight and protected.

Football Hold

Use this hold when you need one hand free.

1 After lifting the infant to the cradle hold position, move the infant to one side. Place the infant's hip on your hip so you can see his or her face.

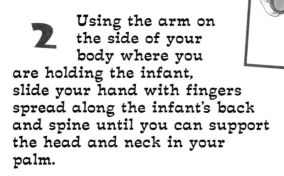

2 Using the arm on the side of your body where you are holding the infant, slide your hand with fingers spread along the infant's back and spine until you can support the head and neck in your palm.

3 Clasp your elbow to your side to hold the infant firmly to your side.

You mean I have to carry something else?!

Shoulder Hold

1 Hold the infant in an upright position so that he or she can look over your shoulder.

2 Put one arm under the infant's bottom and, with the other arm, support the head, neck and back.

Picking Up and Holding Toddlers

◆ If you can support their weight, toddlers like to be held and carried. It is important that you don't lift a toddler who is too heavy for you.

◆ Hold toddlers on your lap when giving them a bottle or a drink from a spill-proof cup or when reading to them.

◆ Toddlers may crawl off your lap if they want to play or if they see something they want to investigate.

◆ Ask toddlers to help when you need to carry them. Toddlers can put both arms around your neck to hold on securely.

Upright Carry for Toddlers

1 Bend your knees.

2 Pick up the toddler under both arms.

3 Carry toddlers from one place to another in an upright position.

4 Put one arm under the toddler's bottom and support his or her back with your other arm.

FEEDING
• • •

Bottle-Feeding

◆ Ask the parents or guardians about feeding their infant. (See the Family Interview Form, pages 13–17.) Infants and toddlers may drink milk, formula, fruit juices or water from a bottle.

◆ NEVER heat a bottle in a microwave. Run the bottle under warm water to bring it to room temperature rather than microwaving. You can also place the bottle in a pot of hot water to bring it to room temperature. Remove the pot from the heat source and turn off the heat source before placing the bottle in the pot. Watch the bottle carefully; only leave it in the water for several minutes.

1 Wash your hands.

2 Keep the infant safe and comfortable. Choose a safe, quiet place for feeding.

3 Gather supplies (bottle, nipple, bib or cloth to protect the infant's clothing; towel or cloth to put over your shoulder for burping the infant).

4

Warm and prepare the bottle as the parent or guardian directed. Gently shake the bottle to make sure it is evenly heated before giving it to the infant. Test the temperature on your wrist. It should be just about skin temperature.

5

Rest the infant comfortably on your lap. Be sure to keep the infant's head higher than his or her shoulders to prevent choking. Put the bib or cloth under the infant's chin and place a towel or cloth on your lap or shoulder to protect your clothes.

6

Give the infant the bottle. Hold the bottle for the infant, unless the infant is old enough to hold it. Carefully watch the bottle as the infant suckles so that air is not getting into the nipple. Keep the infant's head above his or her body.

7

Gently burp the infant when he or she has taken about one third of the bottle. Hold the infant upright and put his or her head on your shoulder.

8

Pat the infant gently on the back until you hear a burp. Some infants spit up a little when burped. You can also burp the baby by sitting him or her on your lap, making sure you support him or her, and patting gently on the back. Burp the infant again when he or she is finished drinking.

Spoon-Feeding

1 Wash your hands and the infant's or toddler's hands.

2 Gather supplies (dish, food, infant/toddler spoon and bib). Put the food in a dish and place the bib under the infant's or toddler's chin.

3 If the infant or toddler uses a high chair or infant seat, get the food ready before you put the child into the chair or seat. Buckle the safety belt securely.

4 Use a spoon to feed an infant strained food or cereal. Test the temperature of the food. Put only a small amount of food on the tip of the spoon. Infants who are just beginning to eat from a spoon may seem to be pushing the food away. Be patient and keep feeding them as long as they seem interested.

5 Wash the infant's or toddler's hands and face and wipe up any food that was spilled when you are done feeding.

6 Wash your hands.

Spoon-Feeding Older Infants and Toddlers

◆ You can heat food by placing the container of food into a container of hot water. If you use a microwave to heat the food, be sure to stir the food well and test the temperature before giving it to an infant or toddler. Put a small amount of food on your wrist to make sure it's cool enough. Lukewarm food won't burn the child's mouth.

◆ Don't blow on food to cool it. Let it cool by itself.

◆ Let toddlers try to feed themselves with the spoon or their hands if they want, even if they make a mess. Help toddlers as needed.

Feeding Preschoolers and School-Aged Children

◆ Follow the parents' or guardians' instructions on what, how much and how to feed the child. (See the Family Interview Form, pages 13–17.)

◆ Most young children eat with their fingers, although some will use a small fork or spoon. Eating is fun for most children. Don't worry if they are messy.

◆ If the child does not eat much or refuses to eat or drink, wait a few minutes and try again. If the child is playing with the food more than eating, the child has probably finished eating.

◆ Older children can feed themselves, but you will need to prepare their food. Let them pitch in by helping you set the table.

Food and Kitchen Safety

◆ Wash your hands before you prepare food.

◆ Wash raw fruits and vegetables carefully before eating them or feeding them to children.

◆ Be careful when using a microwave. Stir foods well after removing them from the microwave. Always test the temperature of foods and drinks before giving them to children.

◆ Never leave a child alone in a high chair — not even for a moment. Keep high chairs away from stoves and counters.

◆ Always use the safety straps on highchairs or booster seats to secure children.

◆ If you must use the stove, put a young child in a safe play area. Use only the back burners and turn pan handles away from the edge of the stove.

◆ Don't let children play in the kitchen.

◆ Follow the parents' directions for cleaning up and putting away unfinished food and drinks.

◆ Avoid foods that are choking hazards for infants or toddlers such as raisins, popcorn, nuts, hard candy, grapes, hotdog slices, etc. Make sure food is cut into small bite-size pieces.

DiAPERiNG
● ● ●

Disposable Diapers

1 Wash your hands.

2 Put on disposable gloves.

3 Gather supplies (two diapers, baby wipes, cleaning materials and plastic trash bag).

4 Keep the infant or toddler safe and comfortable. Use the floor or crib, protected with a water-resistant pad, to change the infant or toddler if you are not comfortable using a changing table.

5 Never leave an infant or toddler alone on a changing table. Even newborn infants turn and squirm when they are being changed and can easily wiggle off the changing table and get hurt. Be sure to use the safety straps or guardrails on a changing table to secure the infant or toddler. Some infants or toddlers are easier to change if they have a toy to hold.

6 Place the infant or toddler on his or her back. Take off the dirty diaper by lifting his or her legs and hips high enough to slide the dirty diaper away. Fold the diaper so that the mess is on the inside. Set the dirty diaper out of the way where the infant or toddler can't reach it. Lift him or her up and clean with baby wipes or a washcloth. Always clean from the front to the back, and be sure to separate the folds of the skin to remove all the mess. Be gentle. When changing a boy, keep him covered with a baby wipe or a diaper as much as possible during the change to avoid being sprayed.

7 Use one hand to hold the infant's or toddler's feet and lift up the bottom. Use the other hand to slip the open clean diaper under his or her bottom. Disposable diapers go on only one way and usually have pictures or cartoons on the front part. Use the cartoon band as a guide to put the diaper on correctly.

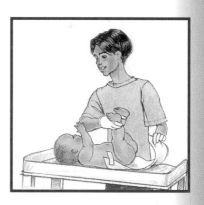

8 Fasten the diaper with the tabs. Put your fingers between the diaper and the infant or toddler so that you don't tape the diaper to him or her.

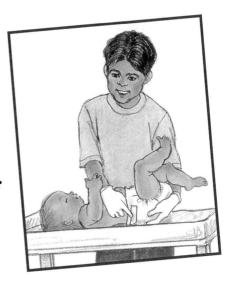

9 Properly dispose of the dirty diaper and baby wipes in the trash, preferably using a plastic trash bag. Keep one hand on the infant or toddler at all times. Make sure the changing surface is clean. Remove your disposable gloves and put them in the plastic trash bag. (See page 62 for how to remove gloves.)

10 Wash the infant's or toddler's hands and place him or her in a safe place while you wash your hands.

I like to keep my paws clean.

Cloth Diapers

1 Wash your hands.

2 Put on disposable gloves.

3 Gather supplies (two diapers, two diaper pins, baby wipes, cleaning materials, plastic trash bag and diaper pail).

4 Fold the diaper for a boy or a girl.

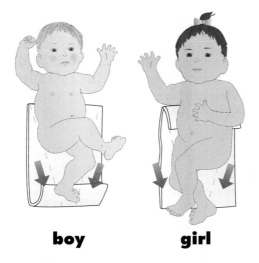

boy   **girl**

5 Remove rubber pants. Unfasten and remove the pins from the diaper, keeping the pins away from the infant or toddler. You can stick the pins in a bar of soap or a pin cushion, but don't put them in your mouth.

6 Keep the infant or toddler safe and comfortable. Use the floor or crib, protected with a water-resistant pad, to change the infant or toddler if you're not comfortable using a changing table.

7 Never leave an infant or toddler alone on a changing table. Even newborn infants turn and squirm when they are being changed and can wiggle off the changing table and get hurt. Be sure to use the safety straps or guardrails on a changing table to secure the infant or toddler. Some infants or toddlers are easier to change if they have a toy to hold.

8 Place the infant or toddler on his or her back. Take off the dirty diaper by lifting his or her legs and hips high enough to slide the dirty diaper away. Fold the diaper so that the mess is on the inside. Set the dirty diaper out of the way where the infant or toddler can't reach it. Lift him or her up and clean with baby wipes or a washcloth. Always clean from the front to the back and be sure to separate the folds of the skin to remove all mess. Be gentle. When changing a boy, keep him covered with a baby wipe or a diaper as much as possible to avoid being sprayed.

9 Use one hand to hold the infant's or toddler's feet and lift up the bottom. Use the other hand to slip the open, clean diaper under his or her bottom. Put the clean diaper under the infant or toddler with the folded part in front for a boy and in back for a girl.

10 Pull the diaper up between the infant's or toddler's legs. Overlap the back of the diaper on top of the front at his or her hips. Hold your fingers between the diaper and the infant or toddler and pin on the outside of the diaper. The diaper should fit snugly but not bind. Put the rubber pants on over the diaper. Keep one hand on the infant or toddler at all times.

11 Dispose of the feces in the toilet and then put the dirty diaper into the diaper pail. Make sure the changing surface is clean. After properly disposing of the dirty baby wipes, remove your disposable gloves and put them in the plastic trash bag. (See page 62 for how to remove gloves.)

12 Wash the infant's or toddler's hands and place him or her in a safe place while you wash your hands.

REMOVING GLOVES

1

Pinch one glove at the wrist and remove it about two thirds of the way, turning it inside out.

2

Pinch the second glove at the wrist.

3

Remove the second glove, turning it inside out.

4

Finish removing both gloves.

5

Discard gloves in an appropriate container. (See the Family Interview Form, pages 13–17, for the proper place to put used gloves.)

6 Wash your hands.

Tearless Toileting Tips

◆ Some older toddlers and most preschoolers are learning to use the toilet. Follow the parents' or guardians' routine and ask what words or signals children use to tell that they "have to go to the bathroom." (See the Family Interview Form, pages 13–17.)

◆ Wash your hands before and after helping the child use the toilet. Be sure children wash their hands after toileting.

◆ Some families have a child-size toilet seat. Some children sit on a full-sized toilet seat.

◆ Children who are already toilet trained sometimes still need help. They may need help unfastening their clothes, wiping themselves or washing their hands. If you help a girl with wiping, wipe from front to back. Be sure girls always wipe from front to back, to keep from spreading germs.

◆ Never make a big deal out of an accident because it might embarrass the child. Clean the child and say it was a good try. Be sure to wear disposable gloves when cleaning the child.

◆ Encourage children to use the toilet often. Give children an opportunity to use the toilet before and after eating, before and after bed, and before and after activities such as playing outside. If children are showing signs that they need to use the bathroom, such as clutching at their pants, shivering or jumping around, take them to the bathroom immediately.

Dogs have it easy with housebreaking!

DRESSING CHILDREN
● ● ●

◆ Ask the parents or guardians about dressing their children. (See Family Interview Form, pages 13–17.)

◆ Give yourself enough time to change the child. Rushing makes the job more difficult and can upset the child.

◆ Let toddlers help with dressing by encouraging them to pull off their socks or pull a loose shirt over their heads. Let them help you undo snaps or buttons.

◆ When dressing an infant, be sure to keep him or her safe and comfortable.

Dressing Safety

◆ Don't let children walk around on uncarpeted surfaces in socks without slip-proof bottoms.

◆ To help prevent children from tripping, do not dress them in pants that are too long. If pants are too long, be sure to roll up the pant legs. Make sure shoes fit securely.

◆ Avoid dressing children in clothes that fasten with drawstrings, especially around the neck. A child can be strangled by a hooded sweatshirt with a drawstring tie that catches on something.

◆ Never leave an infant alone on the changing table.

UNDRESSING CHILDREN

1

Undo the snaps or buttons on the front of the shirt.

2

If the child is wearing a T-shirt or pullover shirt, gently slide one arm out of the sleeve and then slide out the other. Then, ease the shirt over the child's head, gently past one ear, then the other.

3

When undressing an infant, be sure to keep him or her safe and comfortable. Never leave the infant alone on the changing table.

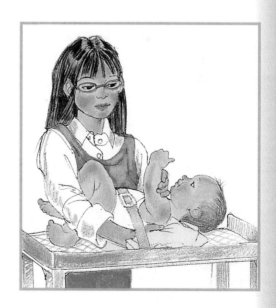

DRESSING SKILLS

● ● ●

Button Shirt

1

To put on a button shirt, open all snaps or buttons. Roll or scrunch-up the sleeves. Reach through one sleeve, grasp the child's hand and draw the hand and arm gently through the sleeve. Bring the shirt around the back of the child. Do the same with the other arm. Fasten the shirt.

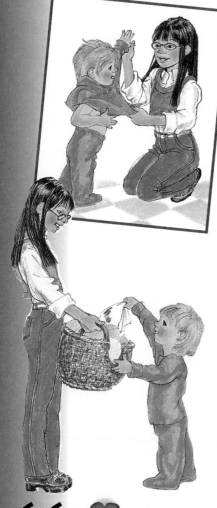

T-shirt

2

To put on a T-shirt or pullover shirt, stretch the neck of the shirt so that it is larger than the child's head. Pull the neck opening over the head, keeping it away from the child's ears and face.

3

Reach through a sleeve opening and gently draw one arm through it. Repeat on the other side. Always be careful to protect the child's eyes, ears, nose and jaw.

4

Put the dirty laundry where the parents or guardians told you to put it. (See the Family Interview Form, pages 13–17.)

REST AND SLEEP

● ● ●

◆ Ask the parents or guardians about the child's nap, rest and bedtime routines. (See the Family Interview Form, pages 13–17.)

◆ Help prepare the child for sleep by choosing quiet activities. Quiet activities include reading comforting stories and listening to soft music.

◆ Some children wake up or come out of quiet time in a calm way. Other children wake up noisy and ready to play.

Quiet time is my favorite time... I could use a nap now!

Putting Children to Bed

1 About 15 minutes ahead of time, tell the child that bedtime or naptime is coming.

2 Check an infant's crib to remove toys, blankets, pillows or any other soft, fluffy objects that could choke or suffocate the infant. (See the Safety Inspection Checklist, pages 91–92, for more bedtime safety tips.)

3 Massaging or rubbing the child's back can be a comforting way to help the child get to sleep.

4 Put infants to sleep on their backs, face-up. It is not safe for infants to sleep on their stomachs or face-down.

5 Tell the child to sleep well and say good night.

6 Check on the child every half-hour. Make sure you stay where you are able to hear the children if they wake up.

7 Put children back to bed if they get up. Comfort them if they are scared or have nightmares. Be kind but firm in helping children stick to their rest and sleep routines.

I love to sleep on my back!

Sudden Infant Death Syndrome (SIDS)

Sudden Infant Death Syndrome (SIDS) is the sudden, unexpected and unexplained death of apparently healthy babies. It is the major cause of death of infants between the ages of 1 month and 1 year. In the United States, SIDS causes the deaths of about 3,000 infants every year. Infants who sleep on their stomachs during the night or naptime have an increased risk of SIDS. To help reduce the risk of SIDS, **always place an infant on his or her back at night or naptime,** using a firm mattress in a (safety-approved) crib or bassinet. Make sure that there is no soft bedding such as pillows or blankets or soft toys such as stuffed animals in the crib or bed. These items could cause suffocation.

BASIC CARE

• • •

"Factoid" Challenge

You are the navigator. Your mission is to search through the following statements to identify the "factoids" (true statements) from the "decoys" (false statements). Circle the "factoids," and cross out the "decoys."

1 Wait until you begin basic care to find out what supplies you need.

2 All children like to be held and cuddled.

3 Let a child sleep with a light on if he or she wants.

4 Put an infant face-down to sleep.

5 Let children eat with their hands if they want.

6 When children wet their pants or the bed, make a big deal out of it so they will remember never to do it again.

7 All families give basic care to their children in the same way.

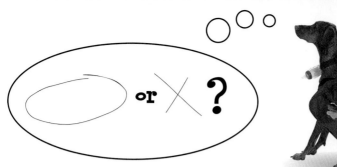

○ or ✕ ?

8 Play an active game and run outdoors with the children just before their bedtime so they'll be tired and want to go to bed.

9 It is normal for children to begin toilet training as early as 2 years and to complete toilet training as old as 5 years.

10 A clean floor is a safe place to change children's diapers and to put on their clothes.

11 Ask children frequently and regularly if they need to use the bathroom.

12 Wash the children's hands, if they are dirty, after changing their diapers.

13 Feed the children yourself because letting them feed themselves takes too long and makes a big mess.

Answers are found on page 159!

STOP: THINK SAFETY!

● ● ●

Safety First

As a babysitter, your biggest responsibility is to keep infants and children safe while their parents or guardians are away. To prevent injuries, watch out for safety-related problems. If you find a safety-related problem, try and use caution to reduce the chance of an injury or illness happening.

Inside and around the home, think about how you can prevent:

◆ Bites and stings;

◆ Burns;

◆ Choking;

◆ Strangulation;

◆ Drowning;

◆ Falls;

◆ Fires;

◆ Illnesses;

◆ Poisoning;

◆ Riding toy/vehicle injuries;

◆ Safety-related problems outdoors;

◆ Wounds; and

◆ Safety-related problems in special environments.

Be a Good Role Model

◆ Children see how you act and imitate you.

◆ Follow the parents' or guardians' guidelines for safe sleep and play.

◆ Use appropriate verbal and non-verbal language.

◆ Wash your hands and keep food areas clean.

- Be aware of possible safety-related problems wherever you are.
- Know how to use the First Aid Action Plans if an injury or illness occurs.
- Wear proper protective gear (such as helmets and pads) when participating in outdoor activities with children, such as when riding bicycles, scooters or roller blading.

Preventing Injuries and Illnesses

- Think safety.
- Fix or remove the safety-related problem if it is safe to do so or keep children away from a dangerous situation.
- Use safety.
- Give care if an emergency does occur (see "First Aid Action Plans" on page 118 for more information).

Think Safety

- Use the Family Interview Form, pages 13–17, and the Safety Inspection Checklist, pages 91–92, to learn about any safety-related problems around the home.
- Check the home and surrounding areas before starting the job.
- Ask the parents or guardians about special safety equipment, such as child-resistant locks or latches for drawers, doors, windows and medicine cabinets; smoke alarms; carbon monoxide alarms; and security devices.
- Ask the parents or guardians to make sure that any guns and ammunition are locked separately and keys are hidden away.
- Stay alert. Supervise children closely to prevent injuries while you are on the job.
- Check that all electrical outlets have safety covers.
- Make sure the parents or guardians teach you about any equipment for children with special needs. Make sure you have an opportunity to practice and feel comfortable using any equipment before the parents or guardians leave.
- Keep the Babysitter's Training Handbook in the Babysitter's Training Safety and First Aid Kit and take them to your babysitting jobs. The kit also contains first aid supplies.
- Use your Babysitter's Report Record, pages 40–42, to let the parents or guardians know about any safety-related problems.

Fix the Safety-Related Problem

◆ Pick up lint, coins, buttons and any small objects from the floor to avoid choking hazards.

◆ Ask the parents or guardians to lock up or remove anything that could poison or harm a child. Again, this would include any guns and ammunition.

◆ Keep toys with small parts away from young children.

◆ Put away broken toys or toys with sharp edges. Notify parents of any broken toys.

◆ Keep cords or strings longer than 12 inches away from infants and small children.

◆ Shut doors to bathrooms and other rooms where a child could get hurt.

◆ Lock doors and gates leading to home swimming pools.

Use Safety

◆ Teach safety in a positive way; use "do" instead of "don't."

◆ Give children safe and real choices.

◆ Know the Family Fire Escape Plan or discuss this with the parents or guardians if there isn't one in place.

◆ Teach and practice good health practices, such as handwashing.

Give Care

◆ Provide care if an emergency occurs. Refer to the First Aid Action Plans, which begin on page 118.

I always refer to my First Aid Action Plans in case of an Emergency!

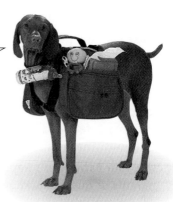

BiTES AND STiNGS

Think Safety

◆ Know what animals and insects are common to your area and how to avoid them.

◆ Find out in advance whether any of the children have allergic reactions to insect bites or stings. If so, find out what to do in case of bites or stings.

Fix the Safety-Related Problem

◆ Keep children from digging or reaching into areas where these animals or insects may live, such as in woodpiles, near garbage, under logs and in leaves or brush.

Use Safety

◆ Keep away from any wild animal or pet that is acting strangely.

◆ Use appropriate insect repellent that has been approved by the parents or guardians to help keep biting insects away.

◆ Have children dress appropriately if playing in or near wooded areas.

Give Care

◆ If a bite or sting does occur, see the First Aid Action Plans for Bites and Stings, page 124.

BURNS

Think Safety

◆ A child can be burned by anything that is hot, including food, water, table lamps, heaters and stoves or ovens.

Fix the Safety-Related Problem

◆ Keep all hot liquids away from infants and children. A child can be scalded by hot water.

◆ Test the temperature of hot bottles and foods before feeding infants and children.

◆ Keep children away from all sources of heat; check rooms carefully for all potential burn risks.

Use Safety

◆ Turn pot handles toward the back of the stove, out of the reach of children.

◆ Don't let children play with safety covers on electrical outlets.

◆ Keep appliance cords out of reach of children.

◆ NEVER hold a child and cook at the same time.

◆ Don't let children climb on stoves or cooking surfaces.

◆ Always use hot pads or oven mitts to remove pots and pans from the stove or oven.

◆ Always place hot items out of the reach of children.

◆ NEVER use a microwave to warm a bottle for an infant; hot spots can form that could potentially burn the infant.

◆ If you use a microwave to warm solid food, stir it and make sure to test the temperature.

◆ Make sure you and the children use sunscreen for outdoor activities, stay out of direct sunlight or wear protective clothing (a hat, a long-sleeved shirt, pants and sunglasses).

Give Care

◆ If a burn does occur, see the First Aid Action Plan for Burns, page 126.

CHOKING AND BREATHING DANGERS

Choking is an emergency in which an infant or child cannot cough, speak, cry or breathe because the airway is partially or completely blocked. Note: Be aware and especially careful with infants and toddlers. They can put things in their mouths and can easily choke.

Think Safety

◆ Look around the home and play areas for small objects that could cause choking.

Fix the Safety-Related Problem

◆ Keep away dangers like plastic bags; balloons; small balls, marbles and toys intended for older children; disposable gloves; beads; pebbles; buttons; caps; hairpins; coins; jewelry and other things that can choke or suffocate an infant or child. Remove small objects from a crib.

◆ Remove smothering risks including objects that can wrap around or cover the face of an infant or small child, such as pillows, blankets, cushions and beanbags.

◆ Keep cords on blinds and draperies out of reach to prevent children from accidentally hanging themselves. Never place a diaper bag on a crib.

◆ Don't use soft bedding in a crib. The U.S. Consumer Product Safety Commission, the American Academy of Pediatrics and the National Institute of Child Health and Human Development Back to Sleep Campaign recommend the following: "If using a blanket, put the baby with his or her feet at the foot of the crib. Tuck a thin blanket around the crib mattress, reaching only as far as the baby's chest." (see Sudden Infant Death Syndrome, page 69).

◆ Make sure clothing does not have drawstrings longer than 3 inches. Sleepwear should not have drawstrings at all.

◆ Never place a crib near a window or dresser.

- Avoid foods that can be dangerous for infants and toddlers, for example:
  - Small food items like raisins, popcorn, nuts, hard candy, grapes, chips, hot dog slices, raw vegetables and marshmallows;
  - Large food items that break into small pieces like teething biscuits and cookies; or
  - Sticky foods like peanut butter.

Use Safety

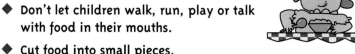

- Always have children sit up when eating.
- Don't let children walk, run, play or talk with food in their mouths.
- Cut food into small pieces.
- Encourage children to take small bites and chew thoroughly.

Give Care

- If choking does occur, see the First Aid Action Plans for Choking, pages 131–132.

DROWNING

A drowning can occur when an infant or child's face is submerged in water (such as a bathtub or toilet bowl) for too long.

Think Safety

◆ Understand that an infant or toddler can drown, at any moment, even in an inch of water.

◆ Do not babysit around pools or other water unless there are trained lifeguards on duty. Even if trained lifeguards are present, you are responsible for the child's safety. Learn about basic water safety (contact your local Red Cross chapter for details on available classes such as GuardStart™).

Fix the Safety-Related Problem

◆ Empty wading pools and cover or secure hot tubs when not in use.

◆ Keep pool gates and patio doors locked.

◆ Keep pool toys stored away.

◆ Empty all water from bathtubs and pails.

Use Safety

◆ Never leave a child alone, even for a moment, in a bathtub or near any water, even a bucket with a small amount of water. If using a bath seat for an infant, NEVER leave the infant. Always stay within arm's reach.

◆ Keep bathroom doors closed and toilet lids down.

◆ Bathe an infant or child only if you have been taught how to do so and you have the approval of the parents or guardians. Never leave an infant or child unattended in or around water.

◆ Be sure trained lifeguards are on duty if you take children swimming. Even at a guarded facility, you are responsible for supervision.

◆ Never trust inflatable flotation devices or bath seats to prevent drowning. Always stay within arm's reach of the child and use Coast Guard approved lifejackets (check for an indication on jacket).

Give Care

◆ If a drowning does occur, see the First Aid Action Plans for Unconscious, Checking an Infant or Child, page 146.

FALLS

Think Safety

◆ Look for anything that could cause an infant or toddler to trip or fall from a height.

Fix the Safety-Related Problem

◆ Keep toys, books, shoes and clutter off the stairs.

◆ Keep the play area free of extra toys.

◆ Keep electric cords and other items away from doors and traffic paths.

Use Safety

◆ Use safety gates and closed doors to keep children from stairs; make the stairways off-limits.

◆ Keep safety rails or sides up on cribs and beds.

◆ NEVER leave an infant alone in a high chair or on a changing table, bed or other high surface. Always use safety straps on high chairs or booster seats to secure the infant or toddler.

◆ Make sure you have access to a working flashlight. Check the batteries frequently.

◆ Put infants on the floor to play, away from stairs and doors.

◆ Keep doors, windows, fences and gates locked.

◆ NEVER let children play near an open window to which they can get access.

Give Care

◆ If a fall does occur, see the First Aid Action Plans, beginning on page 118, to care for the appropriate injury.

FiRE (HEAT SOURCES)

Think Safety

◆ Be careful around any hot items such as stoves, heaters, fireplaces, candles and grills.

Fix the Safety-Related Problem

◆ Keep toys, curtains and similar things away from any hot item.

◆ Keep matches and lighters away from children.

◆ Keep all electrical equipment away from water.

Use Safety

◆ Talk to parents or guardians about a Family Fire Escape Plan.

◆ Learn how and when to use a fire extinguisher and where it is kept. Ask your local fire department for more information.

◆ Teach children to Stop, Drop and Roll if clothing catches on fire.

◆ Teach children to crawl low under smoke and to test for hot doors before opening them.

◆ Know where fire stairs, fire exits and escape ladders are in high-rise buildings and how to use them.

◆ Know where fire alarms and smoke detectors are located.

If Fire Occurs

Your first priority is to get yourself and the children out of the area. NEVER return to a burning building. Your job is to protect the children and yourself, not household belongings. Once you are away from the fire, find the nearest adult or call 9-1-1 or the local emergency number right away!

 iLLNESSES

Think Safety

◆ Although **germs** are present in most places, you can keep them from entering the body and causing illness.

◆ Don't babysit if you feel or are ill.

Fix the Safety-Related Problem

◆ Wash your hands before and after preparing food and after using the restroom, changing diapers, coughing, sneezing or blowing your nose. Always wash your hands after giving first aid.

◆ Make sure infants' and children's hands are washed before and after eating and after toileting or diapering, coughing, sneezing or blowing their nose.

Use Safety

◆ Keep toys clean.

◆ Use tissues and cover mouth and nose when coughing and sneezing.

◆ Keep trash out of the reach of children.

◆ Refrigerate foods that can spoil.

◆ If you or the child touches any animal or its droppings, wash hands well.

Give Care

◆ If illness does occur, use the First Aid Action Plans beginning on page 118 for appropriate care.

Family pets are healthy, clean and child-friendly.

POISONING

Think Safety

◆ Know what items can be poisonous to infants and children.

Fix the Safety-Related Problem

◆ Keep all poisons away from children, including cleaning products, paints, bug and weed killers and car products.

◆ Use disposable gloves if you think you might touch any body fluids, chemicals or poisons from a plant.

◆ Keep children away from alcohol, drugs, medicines, vitamins, lighter fluid, lamp oil, baby oil and tobacco.

◆ Keep children away from plants that they could put into their mouths.

◆ Keep children away from peeling paint or plaster.

Use Safety

◆ If parents ask you to give an infant or child medicine, you and your parents or guardians need to decide if you are comfortable with this responsibility. Discuss this with your parents or guardians before accepting the job.

◆ If parents ask you to give an infant or child medicine, make the child aware that he or she is getting medicine. Don't call it "candy." The parents or guardians should provide clearly written instructions on how to give the medication to the infant or child. Always read the label; make sure it is the right medication and dosage. Record what you gave and when on the Babysitter's Report Record.

◆ Never transfer products and medicines out of child-resistant containers.

◆ Check for safety latches or locks on cabinets and doors where poisonous substances are kept.

◆ Keep children away from cabinets or doors without locks.

- Remember, when using with cleaning products, follow the **BEFORE, WHILE** and **AFTER** rule:
  - **BEFORE** using a cleaning product, read the instructions.
  - **WHILE** using a cleaning product, never leave it alone. A child may find it.
  - **AFTER** using a cleaning product, put it back in a locked cabinet immediately. Make sure the container is closed tightly.

Give Care

- Know the Poison Control Center phone number: (800) 222-1222, or call 9-1-1, the local emergency number or 0 for the operator.
- If a poisoning does occur, see the First Aid Action Plan for Poisoning, page 142.

RIDING TOY/VEHICLE INJURIES

• • •

Think Safety

◆ Accidents with riding toys and motor vehicles can cause serious injuries.

Fix the Safety-Related Problem

◆ Don't let children ride toys near pools, on hilly or steep ground, in streets or on steps.

◆ Don't dress children in clothes with drawstrings, cords or other items that can get caught in wheels or moving parts.

Use Safety

◆ Have children wear a helmet and protective padding (e.g., knee or elbow guards) when using riding toys.

◆ Dress children in bright colors so that they can easily be seen.

◆ Keep children away from curbs, parked cars, hilly areas and streets.

◆ Teach safety rules for crossing the street, including:

◆ Hold hands when crossing the street;

◆ Look both ways before crossing;

◆ Cross only at the crosswalk; and

◆ Teach children not to cross the street without a grown-up or a responsible person, such as a babysitter.

Give Care

◆ If an injury does occur, use the First Aid Action Plans beginning on page 118 for the appropriate care.

SAFETY-RELATED PROBLEMS—PARKS AND OUTDOORS

• • •

Think Safety

◆ Outdoor environments present special hazards and dangers to children that can cause serious injuries or illnesses.

◆ Make sure that the children stay close enough for you to see and hear them.

Fix the Safety-Related Problem

◆ Keep the children away from any unsafe conditions you find.

◆ Dress children and yourself appropriately; for example, tuck pants into socks to protect from the bites of ticks and other insects when playing around wooded, brushy or tall grassy areas.

◆ Check the child and his or her clothing for ticks and other insects before entering the house.

◆ Don't dress the children in garments, such as those with drawstrings and hoods, which could catch on playground equipment.

Use Safety

◆ Check the nearby area for rough spots, holes and any objects that could trip a child.

◆ Watch out for poisonous plants and plants with thorns, stickers, roots that stick up or low branches that could cause scratches.

◆ Check for trash, broken glass, needles, broken cement, animal droppings, sewage and shiny objects, like opened aluminum cans, which can cause wounds.

◆ Check that restrooms are clean and safe for children.

- Inspect play equipment for good condition and look for openings or railings that could trap a child's hands, head or feet (any space larger than the width of a soda can is unsafe).

- Check for sand, wood chips or rubber matting under play equipment to cushion a child's fall.

- Check that the sand in sandboxes is clean and safe for the children to play in.

- Watch out for animals loose in the area.

- Beware of any holes or openings a child could fall into.

- Watch out for storm drains and keep the children away from them, especially after a rainstorm.

- Check for any water in the area, such as a pond or a lake.

- Use appropriate insect repellant that has been approved by the parents or guardians to help keep biting or stinging insects away.

Give Care

- Make sure you have coins or a cell phone for an emergency telephone call to the parents or guardians in case an injury occurs. You do not need to pay to call 9-1-1 or 0 for the operator. If you use a cell phone, make sure you understand how to use it and that the battery is charged. Remember to bring the parent's contact numbers.

WOUNDS

Think Safety

◆ Check toys for sharp edges.

◆ Check rooms and outside play areas for objects or surfaces that could cause harm to a child (including glass and other sharp objects).

Fix the Safety-Related Problem

◆ Remove all sharp objects from children's reach.

◆ Ask parents or guardians to lock up dangerous things like knives, saws, hammers, screwdrivers, power tools and guns, plus ammunition.

Use Safety

◆ Keep children away from large glass doors or windows.

◆ Make sure play areas are safe.

◆ Make sure children always wear shoes when outside playing.

◆ Make sure children wear the right clothing for the weather and use proper protective gear for outdoor activities, such as helmets, knee and elbow pads for bike riding and skate boarding. If you have questions, be sure to ask the parents or guardians.

◆ Closely supervise all play.

Give Care

◆ If a wound does occur, see the First Aid Action Plan for Bleeding, page 125.

BEING PREPARED FOR ENVIRONMENTAL EMERGENCIES

• • •

Check your Family Interview Form, pages 13–17, for the parents' or guardians' instructions in case of an emergency.

Violence or Crime

◆ Be aware of your surroundings and what is going on around you.

◆ Avoid wearing or doing anything that would draw attention to you by dangerous people who may cause you or the children harm.

◆ Know how to open security bars or doors, where emergency exits are located and how to get out of the house or apartment building.

◆ If you hear gunfire, you and the children should lay down on the ground or floor and wait for 20 to 30 minutes before leaving cover; call 9-1-1 or the local emergency number as soon as the scene is safe.

◆ If it looks as if the home has been broken into when you return from an outing, DO NOT enter. Take the children to a safe place, such as a designated neighbor, local business (or a police or fire station) and call 9-1-1 or the local emergency number; then contact the parents right away. Your job is to protect yourself and the children, not household belongings.

Electrical Storms

◆ If you are outside, go inside a safe structure such as a house or building or seek shelter (but do not go under a tree, shed or other yard structure).

◆ Stay off the phone during storms.

◆ Don't shower, bathe or touch water.

◆ Know where working flashlights and extra batteries are kept.

◆ Never use candles; look for safe alternative lighting such as lightsticks or flashlights.

- Turn off and unplug electrical appliances, such as the TV or computer.
- Comfort and keep track of the children during storms and power outages.

Floods, Earthquakes, Tornadoes, Winter Storms and Hurricanes

- Listen to local radio or TV stations for instructions on what to do and where to go.
- Know where to take the children for shelter, especially if you are in a mobile home.
- Know where and how to turn off the power.
- During winter storms, keep children inside and warm.
- Know the family plan in case of storms or natural disasters.
- Know where the disaster supply kit is kept and what's in it; it should be well stocked. Go to the American Red Cross Disaster Services Web site at http://www.disasterrelief.org/Library/Prepare/supplies.html for contents. For information on a variety of training opportunities including disaster preparedness, home and personal safety, contact your local Red Cross chapter for more details.

If you have to take the children to a shelter, let the parents know where you are going (if possible) and try to contact them when you get there.

SAFETY INSPECTION CHECKLIST – CHECK IT OUT! ● ● ●

☐ The emergency phone list has been filled out and is posted

_____
_____
_____
_____.

☐ The first aid kit is properly stocked and stored away

_____
_____
_____
_____.

☐ Working flashlights are located

_____
_____
_____
_____.

☐ The children are not allowed in

_____
_____
_____
_____.

(Examples include garage, basement, office, pool areas)

To Prevent Wounds

☐ Guns, ammunition, knives, hand tools, power tools, razor blades, scissors and other objects that can cause injury are stored in locked cabinets or locked storage areas.

To Prevent Falls

☐ Discourage use of chairs or stools to reach anything high up.

☐ Safety gates are installed at all open stairways.

☐ Windows and balcony doors have childproof latches.

☐ Balconies have protective barriers to prevent children from slipping through bars.

☐ The home is free of clutter on the floors and especially on or near stairways.

To Prevent Poisoning

☐ Potential poisons like detergents, polishes, pesticides, car care fluids, lighter fluids and lamp oils are stored in locked cabinets and are out of the reach of children.

☐ Houseplants are kept out of reach.

☐ Medicine is kept in a locked storage place that children can't reach.

☐ Child-resistant packaging is re-closed securely.

To Prevent Burns

☐ Safety covers are placed on all unused electrical outlets.

☐ Loose cords are secured and out of the way. Multi-cord or octopus plugs are not used. (They may overheat and cause fires.)

☐ At least one approved smoke alarm is installed and operating on each level of the house.

☐ Space heaters are placed out of the reach of children and away from curtains.

☐ Flammable liquids are securely stored in their original containers.

☐ Matches and lighters are stored out of the reach of children.

☐ Garbage and recycling materials are stored in covered containers.

☐ The children in the house know and have practiced a Family Fire Escape Plan.

To Prevent Drowning

☐ Swimming pools and hot tubs are completely enclosed with a barrier, such as a locked fence, gate and cover.

☐ Wading pools and bathtubs are emptied when not in use.

☐ The toilet seat and lid are kept down when not in use.

☐ The bathroom door is kept closed at all times.

☐ Stay within an arm's length of a child in any situation involving water.

☐ 5-gallon buckets or other containers with standing water are securely covered or emptied of water.

To Prevent Choking and Other Breathing Dangers

☐ The toy box has ventilation holes and if it has a lid, it is a light-weight removable lid, a sliding door or panel, or a hinged lid with a support to hold it open.

☐ The crib mattress fits the side of the crib snugly and toys, blankets and pillows are removed from the crib.

☐ Always put an infant on his or her back (not the stomach) and in a crib to sleep.

☐ Small objects are kept out of children's reach.

SAFETY SEARCH!

SAFETY SEARCH!
ACTIVITY PAGE
● ● ●

Look for safety-related problems in the house on the previous page. Then, circle the problem; note how you would fix it and how you would use safety in the columns on this page.

Safety-Related Problem	How to Fix It	How to Use Safety

LESSON 5

SAFE PLAY

Play It Safe!

Keep children safe during play by watching them at all times. While you play with the children, watch how they act, learn what activities they like best and discover how they want to play.

◆ Follow the family's rules for play. (See the Family Interview Form, pages 13–17.)

◆ Choose the right toys and games for each child, based on his or her age and likes and dislikes. Safety depends on the right toy and activity at the right age.

◆ Actively play with the children—don't just watch them.

Why Should You Play With Children?

◆ Playing with children makes it easy to supervise them and to remove any safety-related problems from the area.

◆ Playing allows you to show them how to behave during play, praise good behavior, as well as control any behavior problems.

◆ Playing is fun for both you and the children and helps you feel you've done a good job as a babysitter.

How Can You Help Children Play?

◆ Respect their likes and dislikes when choosing toys and games.

◆ Be truly interested and involved in their play.

Be a Good Role Model

◆ Be aware of safety in all activities.

◆ Wash your hands and keep toys and play areas clean.

◆ Cheerfully resolve any problems that arise during play.

◆ Enjoy playing with the children.

Why Should Children Play?

◆ Playing helps children develop physically. Running, jumping, dancing, putting beads on a string and coloring—all of these help children grow.

◆ Playing helps children improve their learning skills. Learning rhymes, singing songs, doing puzzles, sorting and naming things, counting and reading—all of these help children learn.

◆ Playing helps children understand and control their feelings. This may involve banging a drum, play-acting, imagining, asking "what if" questions or playing games with others.

◆ Playing helps children develop socially. Pretending to be someone else, acting out a story, playing team sports, playing an instrument in a band, taking turns jumping rope and playing board games with others—all of these give children stronger social skills.

How Do Children Play?

Children play in different ways as they develop and grow older. You will play in different ways with children at different ages and developmental stages.

◆ Infants first play by themselves.

◆ Older infants play while watching others, but they rarely interact directly with others.

◆ Toddlers may play alongside other toddlers, but they rarely share and play with one another.

◆ As toddlers develop into preschoolers, they play side by side and begin interacting and sharing.

◆ Preschoolers enjoy interacting with one another. A game like Duck-Duck-Goose has simple rules and allows children to interact with each other. Sometimes preschoolers want to make up their own rules.

◆ School-aged children learn to play in an organized way. They take on roles, understand having a leader and play as a team. Rules are very important to them.

CREATE PLAY

Instructions

Toys and games do not need to be expensive to be fun. Use pieces of paper, your 5 senses and household items to create fun games or toys for different ages. Use your imagination and fill in the blanks below!

Refer to Ages and Stages (pages 32–33) and Safety and Toys (pages 98–100) for more ideas!

	Paper	5 Senses	Household Items
Infants	Peekaboo		
Toddlers		Name colors of common objects	
Preschoolers	Make a paper hat		
School-Aged Children			Use paper bags and crayons to make puppets

SAFETY AND TOYS
• • •

Choose the toys that are right for each child. Here are some suggestions.

Infants (Newborn to 6 Months)
Toys

- Soft mobiles
- Rattles
- Soft fabric swatches
- Stuffed animals

Infants (6 Months to 1 Year)
Toys

- Large colored blocks made of rubber or soft material
- Large nesting boxes or cups
- Squeaky toys or bells
- Large balls
- Pots and pans
- Wooden spoons and plastic bowls
- Simple picture books or cloth books
- Push-pull toys
- Teething toys

Note: No toy should be smaller than 1¼ inches in diameter

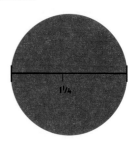

1¼

Activities

- Music of different types
- Reading
- Rhymes
- Hand games like peekaboo or finger play
- Looking at self in mirror

For a free copy of the publication, "Which Toy for Which Child: Ages Birth through 5," write for item #285, or item #286, "Which Toy for Which Child: Ages 6-12," U.S. Consumer Product Safety Commission, Washington, DC 20207. More safety information is available at http://www.cpsc.gov or by calling the Consumer Product Safety Commission's toll-free hotline at (800) 638-2772.

Toddlers (1 to 3 Years)

Toys

- Building blocks
- Large plastic toy people and animals
- Action toys like telephones, trains, planes, cars and trucks
- Simple puzzles with knobs
- Puppets
- Large balls or staple-free cardboard boxes
- Books
- Drums, xylophone and other musical toys
- Pail and shovel
- Riding toys

Activities

- Reading
- Coloring and painting
- Music, dancing and singing
- Sand and water play (if closely supervised)
- Imaginative play
- Storytelling

Preschoolers (3 to 5 Years)

Toys

- Playground equipment: seesaw, swings, slides and climbing structures (if closely supervised)
- Simple board games
- Storybooks
- Balls
- Musical instruments
- Dolls and props for pretend play—cooking, cleaning and carpentry
- Skates, wagons and tricycles
- Puzzles with large pieces
- Sand and water play (if closely supervised)

Activities

- Physically active games—hide-and-seek and follow the leader
- Arts and crafts

**School-Aged Children
(5 Years and Older)
Toys**

- Board games
- Items related to hobbies or collections—stickers, rocks or miniature cars
- Electronic games
- Fashion and action dolls

Activities

- Reading and storytelling
- Hobbies of all kinds:
- Sewing
- Woodworking
- Gardening
- Sports
- Music and dancing
- Arts and crafts

Have enough toys for all the toddlers and they'll play side by side.

TOY BOX JUMBLE

Children play safely with different toys at different ages. On the grid below, you will find 12 toys or activities appropriate for infants, toddlers, preschoolers or school-aged children. Words can be horizontal, vertical, diagonal or backward. Circle the 12 toys or activities. Then, after thinking about who could safely enjoy playing with that toy or activity, put it in the appropriate toy box by writing the word in the box. Think carefully! A few of the toys or activities might go into more than one toy box.

Toys and Activities:
checkers, duck duck goose, mobile, finger paints, tricycle, rattle, skateboard, teething ring, books, stacking rings, peekaboo, basketball

E	E	H	H	S	T	N	I	A	P	R	E	G	N	I	F	G	A	B	O
A	A	Z	R	S	S	T	T	Y	L	E	P	P	Q	B	N	M	M	T	B
N	R	R	C	A	N	A	R	C	T	R	I	C	Y	C	L	E	O	H	E
T	J	A	T	T	U	V	H	O	P	G	H	B	E	E	T	J	O	L	N
K	S	T	E	E	T	H	I	N	G	R	I	N	G	B	B	G	C	R	T
L	A	T	D	E	M	C	C	R	S	R	G	B	J	O	D	D	T	D	B
B	I	L	D	N	A	H	H	S	N	T	C	I	I	O	O	S	E	A	D
C	J	E	S	S	E	S	O	O	G	K	C	U	D	K	C	U	D	V	E
S	R	H	E	C	L	H	P	Q	Q	E	I	Q	R	S	E	S	S	V	L
Q	P	H	K	O	O	L	K	L	L	H	O	G	Q	D	A	A	B	S	I
C	K	E	O	B	S	T	A	C	K	I	N	G	R	I	N	G	S	N	B
T	R	P	C	L	H	K	Z	B	Y	Z	M	N	O	P	N	S	S	T	O
S	T	C	C	N	M	J	K	U	T	C	A	F	F	P	K	E	D	K	M
L	Y	E	D	M	D	R	A	O	B	E	T	A	K	S	F	F	O	A	L
R	L	P	E	E	K	A	B	O	O	C	K	O	G	F	F	O	N	M	L
J	E	P	T	M	H	N	F	F	P	C	W	S	M	M	B	I	P	V	K
O	F	G	O	M	E	L	F	G	B	D	W	U	A	T	T	I	Q	J	V
H	C	O	M	M	L	E	A	A	B	N	X	N	S	B	R	A	L	A	K
N	Q	S	P	J	M	S	S	T	O	R	B	O	T	U	P	A	N	K	A

TOY BOX
GAME PAGE
• • •

Infant's Toy Box

TOYS

Toddler's Toy Box

Toys

Preschooler's Toy Box

Toys

School-Aged Toy Box

Toys

Answers are found on page 160!

BASIC FIRST AID
:::

What Is an Emergency?

Babysitters must know what to do in an emergency. An emergency is a situation where action is needed right away. Some emergencies involve calling 9-1-1 or the local emergency number, and some do not. The most important thing to do in any emergency is to stay calm.

How Do You Know It's an Emergency?

A babysitter needs to use his or her senses of sight, smell, touch and hearing to determine whether there is an emergency. For example, you may see something unusual or hear an accident happen or someone call for help. You may smell something that signals a problem, like smoke from a fire. These signals could mean that you need to take action quickly to protect yourself and the children.

What Is an Environmental Emergency?

Environmental emergencies, such as a fire, flood, explosion or poisonous gases, require your immediate action. You may need to call for help or get the children to a safe place.

What Is a First Aid Emergency?

A first aid emergency involves an injury or illness to someone. All first aid emergencies require your immediate action. Some involve calling 9-1-1 or the local emergency number; others do not. For example, a small cut on a child's finger requires your immediate action but not a call to 9-1-1. However, for a life-threatening first aid emergency (such as a child who is not breathing) your action requires calling 9-1-1 or the local emergency number and providing care.

Life-Threatening First Aid Emergencies

Life-threatening emergencies are situations that could cause death quickly if you do not take immediate action. In a life-threatening first aid emergency, you need to give first aid care and call 9-1-1 or your local emergency number. The following first aid emergencies are life threatening:

◆ An infant or child is **unconscious**;

◆ An infant or child is not breathing or is having trouble breathing;

◆ An infant or child has no **signs of circulation** (these include normal breathing, coughing or movement in response to **rescue breaths**);

◆ An infant or child has **severe bleeding** you can't stop; and

◆ An infant or child can't move his or her arms or legs.

For any life-threatening emergency, call 9-1-1 or the local emergency number. If someone is with you, have him or her call.

What to Do in a First Aid Emergency

Stay calm, use the action steps Check-Call-Care. The order of Check-Call-Care may vary slightly based on the emergency situation and who is available to help.

Check the scene
◆ Make sure there is nothing that could hurt you or cause further injury to the infant or child. If there is, get yourself and the children to a safe place.

◆ Look for any clues that may show what happened. You might see something that looks like poison or something that caused an injury.

Check the infant or child
◆ See what is wrong. Tap the infant or child and shout to see if he or she is awake and breathing. You will need to check for life-threatening emergencies first (see the First Aid Action Plan for Checking a Conscious Child or Infant on page 128 for an example).

CALL

◆ In a life-threatening first aid emergency, call 9-1-1 or the local emergency number. If someone is with you, including a child old enough to use the telephone, have him or her call while you provide care.

◆ When alone, Call First, that is call 9-1-1 or the local emergency number before providing care for an unconscious child over 8 years old or under 8 years old with known heart problems.

◆ When alone, Call Fast, that is call 9-1-1 or the local emergency number after providing 1 minute of care for an unconscious child under 8 years old.

◆ If the problem is not life threatening but might get worse soon, call the parents or guardians.

CARE

◆ The care you give depends on the kind of emergency or problem.

◆ Use the First Aid Action Plans, which begin on page 118 of this handbook. These plans will help you take care of the different kinds of injuries and illnesses infants or children may experience.

How to Call for Help

Call 9-1-1 or the local emergency number.

Is 9-1-1 used in your area? _____

If not, write your local emergency phone number here:

_____

The Poison Control Center (PCC) phone number is: (800) 222-1222

Here's how to call:

1 Call 9-1-1 or the local emergency number.

2 Tell the dispatcher who answers the phone that you have an emergency.

3 Answer any questions you are asked, such as who you are, what happened, what is the address (and nearest cross street), the number you are calling from, how many people are injured and what type of care, if any, is being given.

4 Don't hang up! Wait until the dispatcher tells you to hang up. He or she may need more information. The dispatcher might tell you what to do. Follow his or her instructions. The dispatcher will send medical help to your location to give care. An ambulance may arrive first or police or firefighters may come to help if they can get there first.

5 After you call 9-1-1, the local emergency number or the Poison Control Center, call the child's parents or guardians as soon as possible and ask them to return home immediately.

First Aid Kit

Your first aid kit should have items you will need for an emergency. You can make your own or buy one. Always take your first aid kit with you when you babysit. Make sure your first aid kit has the supplies you need and is ready to use. If you take the children away from home, such as to the park or for a walk, take the kit with you (remember, let the parents know where you are going).

Keep the first aid kit away from the children. Some things in the kit can be dangerous for children. If you do not own a first aid kit, ask where the family's first aid kit is located when you are interviewing the parents or guardians. Ask to see the kit and check it out to make sure it has the supplies you might need.

The Babysitter's Training Safety and First Aid Kit is available from your local Red Cross chapter. The kit has the following supplies in it:

◆ Disposable latex gloves (two pairs);

◆ Hand wipes or towelettes (for use when no soap and water is available);

◆ Adhesive bandages in different sizes and shapes (kids like the ones in colors or with pictures on them);

- Gauze pads;
- Roller gauze bandage;
- Emergency Action Steps (wallet card);
- Emergency Numbers and Family Information notepad;
- Pen; and
- Small working flashlight (you need to supply the batteries).

You may want to add the following items to your first aid kit, depending on your needs:

- Adhesive tape in different sizes;
- Safety scissors;
- Pencil;
- Tweezers;
- Breathing barriers for giving rescue breaths;
- Zipper-lock plastic bags;
- Extra disposable gloves (latex and vinyl or nitrile);
- Cell phone or coins for a pay phone;
- Cold pack; and
- Anything else needed for the children you are babysitting.

What Is a Breathing Emergency?

A breathing emergency is when someone is not breathing or is having trouble breathing. If an infant or child has a breathing emergency, you must act fast. The heart will stop soon if the infant or child is not breathing. First aid for a breathing emergency can save the infant's or child's life.

Breathing emergencies can occur for different reasons:

- Choking on an object, such as a piece of food or a small toy;
- An asthma attack;
- An allergic reaction to a bee sting that causes a swollen throat;
- An illness, such as croup, that causes a swollen throat; or
- An electric shock or drowning that causes breathing to stop.

Signals of a Breathing Emergency

The signals of a breathing emergency include:

◆ An infant or child may be restless, dizzy, excited or appear sleepy;

◆ Skin that may be pale, blue or ashen (gray in color);

◆ Lips or fingernails may be blue;

◆ Breathing that may be fast or slow;

◆ Breathing that may be noisy, with the infant or child making sounds, such as wheezing, gurgling or hoarse crying;

◆ An infant or child who may be grasping at his or her throat; and

◆ An infant or child who may be silent but have a surprised, confused or panicked look on the face.

Check to Find Out What the Problem Is

Earlier in this lesson, you learned how to use the action steps Check-Call-Care in an emergency. When an infant or child is having trouble breathing, check him or her quickly to find out:

◆ If he or she can breathe (look for movement or watch to see if the chest rises and falls);

◆ If he or she can cough (if he or she is coughing, don't try to stop him or her; tell the child to keep coughing); and

◆ If he or she can talk or cry.

If the infant or child is coughing or can talk or cry, he or she is conscious and breathing—but still may be having trouble breathing. If a child has a known problem with asthma or croup, follow the parents' instructions in case of an attack. If you are not sure and a child appears to have trouble breathing, call the parents and ask what to do. To help an infant or child with trouble breathing, see the First Aid Action Plans for Choking, Conscious Child, page 131, or Choking, Conscious Infant, page 132, and Checking an Unconscious Infant or Child, page 146.

First Aid for an Infant or Child Who Is Unconscious and Has Stopped Breathing

If an infant or child is unconscious and has stopped breathing, but has some signs of circulation, the first aid care you provide is called "giving rescue breaths." This is a method of blowing air into an infant's or child's mouth and/or nose to get air into the lungs. This method and when to call for help is briefly described in the First Aid Action Plans for Checking an Unconscious Infant or Child, page 146. This care may be needed to save a life.

First Aid for a Child Who Is Unconscious and Is Breathing

If a child is breathing (he or she has a sign of circulation — normal breathing!), you can place the child (not an infant) in a recovery position while you call 9-1-1 or the local emergency number. This method and when to call for help is briefly described in the First Aid Action Plan for Checking an Unconscious Infant or Child, page 146.

Breathing Barriers

You may feel uncomfortable putting your mouth on someone else's to give rescue breaths, especially if it is someone you don't know. It's normal to worry about this. The chance of getting a disease from giving rescue breaths is very low. Using face shields and masks can lower that risk even more. They can also help to protect you from blood and other body fluids.

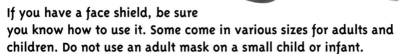

If you have a face shield, be sure you know how to use it. Some come in various sizes for adults and children. Do not use an adult mask on a small child or infant.

You can use a simple face shield that is small enough to fit in your pocket or first aid kit. Place this shield over the infant or child's mouth and breathe through the opening. Other devices include masks with valves.

Keep a breathing barrier with your first aid kit or ask if the family has one. Be sure you learn how to use what you have available. You can buy breathing barriers at your local Red Cross chapter.

Choking

Choking is a common breathing problem in children. A choking infant or child can quickly stop breathing, become unconscious and die. That's why it is important to recognize when an infant or child is choking.

Signals of Choking

An infant or child may be choking if he or she is:

◆ Coughing hard but can't get the object unstuck from the airway;

◆ Coughing weakly or making a high-pitched sound while breathing;

◆ Unable to speak, cry, cough or breathe;

◆ Clutching or grabbing at the throat; or

◆ Unconscious.

For a conscious choking infant or child, the first step is to get the object out and the air in. The care differs for an infant and a child because of the difference in body sizes. The care also differs depending on whether the infant or child is conscious or unconscious. Turn to the First Aid Action Plans for Choking:

◆ Choking, Conscious Child, page 131; and

◆ Choking, Conscious Infant, page 132.

To learn how to care for an unconscious choking victim, take an infant and child CPR class at your local Red Cross chapter.

Bleeding Emergencies

Bleeding is caused by a wound or injury. Infants and children get scrapes and scratches frequently. Blood vessels under the skin are like pipes carrying blood throughout the body. If a blood vessel is torn or damaged, blood is lost.

Bleeding usually stops by itself in a few minutes, but sometimes it does not. The First Aid Action Plan for Bleeding, page 125, tells you how to care for bleeding.

Bleeding that stops by itself in a few minutes is called minor bleeding. With a more serious wound or injury, like a deep cut, severe bleeding may occur and be hard to stop. Blood can squirt from a wound if a larger blood vessel under the skin is damaged. In this case, first aid is needed right away to stop the bleeding.

Types of Wounds

The first aid you give depends on the type of wound:

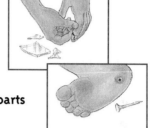

◆ **Scrapes** are the most common type of wound. The skin is rubbed or scraped away, often from a fall. Usually these wounds do not bleed a lot, but they need careful cleaning to prevent infections.

◆ **Cuts** can be caused by sharp objects, such as scissors, knives or broken glass. These wounds sometimes cause a lot of bleeding.

◆ **Avulsions** are where the skin or body parts have been partially or completely torn away.

◆ **Puncture wounds** happen when a pointed object, like a nail, needle or a knife, pierces deep through the skin. These wounds bleed very little and are prone to infection.

◆ **Burns** are caused by heat, chemicals, electricity and the sun. The burn can appear red, brown, black or white; it may swell and be painful. If an infant or child in your care gets burned, call 9-1-1 or the local emergency number.

DECISION MAKING IN EMERGENCIES

● ● ●

Emergency 1

Twelve-year-old Alex is babysitting 6-year-old twin brothers, Jake and Joey. Alex decides to take the boys to a neighborhood park for a bike ride. As he is leading the boys across a busy road on the way to the park, Alex hears screeching tires and then hears Joey fall from his bike, screaming in pain. Alex stops, puts his bike on the side of the road and tells Jake to do the same and to stay on the curb. Joey is lying on the road, clearly injured. He says, "I hit a rock and lost control of my bike and now I can't move my leg." His right pant leg is torn and his knee is bloody. Joey is clearly very frightened. What should Alex do?

Pretend that you are Alex.

1 Is it safe?

2 Check the scene. What happened? How can you tell?

3 Are the other children safe while you attend to the emergency? How do you know? If they are not, what should you do?

4 Check the infant or child. Is he or she conscious or unconscious? How do you know?

5 Is the infant or child breathing? How do you know?

6 Is the infant or child coughing or showing any kind of movement when you give a rescue breath? How do you know?

7 Is the infant or child bleeding severely? How do you know?

8 Should you call anyone about this emergency?

Who?

Why?

When?

9 What should you do after making the call?

10 How could this situation have been prevented?

DECISION MAKING iN EMERGENCIES
• • •

Emergency 2

Fourteen-year-old Maria is babysitting her 8-year-old sister, Anna. Anna is helping Maria make lunch. Maria asks Anna to carry the sandwich plate to the table across the kitchen, but instead Anna picks up the soup bowl, spilling hot soup on her hands and arms. When Maria hears the bowl break and her sister yell, she goes to check on Anna who is crying. Maria sees that a small area of skin on Anna's left arm has turned bright red. What should Maria do?

Pretend that you are Maria.

1 Is it safe?

2 Check the scene. What happened? How can you tell?

3 Are the other children safe while you attend to the emergency? How do you know? If they are not, what should you do?

4 Check the infant or child. Is he or she conscious or unconscious? How do you know?

5 Is the infant or child breathing? How do you know?

6 Is the infant or child coughing or showing any kind of movement when you give a rescue breath? How do you know?

7 Is the infant or child bleeding severely? How do you know?

8 Should you call anyone about this emergency?

    Who?

    Why?

    When?

9 What should you do after making the call?

10 How could this situation have been prevented?

DECISION MAKING IN EMERGENCIES

• • •

Emergency 3

Thirteen-year-old Ted is babysitting 3-year-old Johnny and 8-year-old Greg. Ted makes hot dogs and applesauce for lunch for the boys and himself. He cuts Johnny's hot dog into small pieces before putting the boys' plates in front of them. When Ted looks away, Johnny grabs a piece of hot dog from Greg's plate and tries to eat the bigger piece that Greg cut for himself. Johnny is having trouble swallowing the large bite and looks afraid. He isn't talking or coughing and when Ted shouts his name, Johnny begins grabbing at his throat. What should Ted do?

Pretend that you are Ted.

1 Is it safe?

2 Check the scene. What happened? How can you tell?

3 Are the other children safe while you attend to the emergency? How do you know? If they are not, what should you do?

4 Check the infant or child. Is he or she conscious or unconscious? How do you know?

5 Is the infant or child breathing? How do you know?

6 Is the infant or child coughing or showing any kind of movement when you give a rescue breath? How do you know?

7 Is the infant or child bleeding severely? How do you know?

8 Should you call anyone about this emergency?

Who?

Why?

When?

9 What should you do after making the call?

10 How could this situation have been prevented?

DECISION MAKING IN EMERGENCIES
● ● ●

Emergency 4

Twelve-year-old Amanda is babysitting 11-month-old Greta. Amanda goes to answer the phone. Greta is out of her sight for less than a minute. When she returns, Greta is lying strangely on the floor and does not respond when Amanda calls her name and gently touches her. What should Amanda do?

Pretend that you are Amanda.

1 Is it safe?

2 Check the scene. What happened? How can you tell?

3 Are the other children safe while you attend to the emergency? How do you know? If they are not, what should you do?

4 Check the infant or child. Is he or she conscious or unconscious? How do you know?

5 Is the infant or child breathing? How do you know?

6 Is the infant or child coughing or showing any kind of movement when you give a rescue breath? How do you know?

7 Is the infant or child bleeding severely? How do you know?

8 Should you call anyone about this emergency?

Who?

Why?

When?

9 What should you do after making the call?

10 How could this situation have been prevented?

FIRST AID PUZZLE

• • •

Complete the crossword puzzle, using the words missing in these first aid sentences.

a. Most important in any _ _ _ _ _ _ _ _ _: Stay calm.

b. Scrapes and a _ _ _ are examples of types of wounds.

c. An emergency is a problem situation where _ _ _ _ _ _ is needed right away because someone is injured or ill or there is danger.

d. To call for help in an emergency, call _ _ _ or your _ _ _ _ _ emergency phone number.

e. Keep your first aid kit away from _ _ _ _ _ _ _ _.

f. If an infant or child has _ _ _ _ _ _ _ breathing, the first aid you give is called "giving rescue breaths."

g. An infant or child may be choking if he or she is unable to speak, cry, _ _ _ _ _ or breathe.

h. _ _ _ _ _ _ bleeding is a life-threatening emergency.

Use the list below to help you select the correct words to complete the puzzle.

Bites	Poison	Local
Severe	Cough	Stopped
Infants	Wheezing	Choking
Safety	Children	Action
Emergency	9-1-1	Cut
Minor		

Use your first aid knowledge to solve this puzzle quicker than I can wag my tail!

116

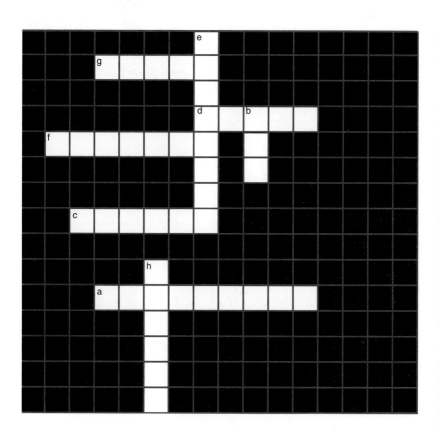

Look at the answer key if you tried but still need help.

Answers are found on page 159!

FIRST AID ACTION PLANS

• • •

CONTENTS

Special Note: This course does not provide certification in first aid or CPR. It does, however, provide you with some knowledge and skill practice in these areas. For additional life-saving information or certification in CPR or first aid, contact your local Red Cross chapter.

Emergency Action Steps

CHECK

CALL

CARE

Allergic Reactions

Notes

- Allergic reactions can be caused by certain foods, animals, chemicals, medications, bites, stings or poisonous plants.
- They may cause swelling of the face, neck and tongue.
- They may cause trouble breathing and make the chest and throat feel tight.
- They may cause rashes, hives or itching.
- The child may feel dizzy or confused.

First Aid Steps

CHECK the scene and the infant or child. Decide whether the area is safe. Use disposable gloves if you think you might touch any body fluids, chemicals or poisons from a plant.

CALL 9-1-1 or the local emergency number, or have someone else call, if the infant or child shows any of the following signals:

- Trouble breathing;
- Uncontrollable coughing or wheezing;
- Tightness in the chest or throat; or
- Swelling of the face, neck or tongue.

CARE for the infant or child:

- Help the infant or child into a position that is comfortable for breathing.
- Provide the infant or child with his or her prescribed medication as directed by the parents or guardians.
- ◆ Call the parents or guardians if the infant or child has:
  - Hives;
  - Pale, gray or flushed skin;
  - An itchy rash that is spreading;
  - Nausea or vomiting; and
  - Swelling.
- ◆ Provide care until the ambulance personnel or the parents or guardians arrive and take over.
- ◆ Fill out the Babysitter's Report Record (pages 40–42).
- ◆ Report to the parents or guardians when they arrive.

See also Vomiting, page 148.

Bites, Animal and Human

Notes (Animal Bites)

- Get the infant or child away from the animal if you can do it safely.

- Don't try to catch or touch the animal.

- Try to remember what the animal looked like and where you saw it last.

- Remind the parents or guardians to report the bite to the local authorities (animal control officer or other law enforcement officer) unless it is a family pet.

Note (Human Bites)

- A human bite can cause serious infection.

First Aid Steps

CHECK the scene and the infant or child. Decide whether the area is safe for you to enter. Use disposable gloves if you think you might touch any body fluids.

CALL 9-1-1 or the local emergency number, or have someone else call, if the wound is large or deep or bleeds severely.

CARE for the infant or child:

- Stop the bleeding (see Bleeding, page 125).
- If the wound is minor:
  - Wash the bite area with soap and water.
  - If the skin was broken, cover the bite with a dressing and bandage.
  - Help the infant or child rest comfortably.

- ◆ If the skin was broken or if the child is upset, call the parents or guardians and ask them to return home immediately.

- ◆ Provide care until the ambulance personnel or the parents or guardians arrive and take over. Tell the ambulance personnel what happened when they ask.

- ◆ Fill out the Babysitter's Report Record (pages 40–42).

- ◆ Report to the parents or guardians when they arrive.

See also Bleeding, page 125.

Bites, Snake

Note

- Do not try to catch the snake; remember what it looked like and tell this to the Poison Control Center. They can call for an ambulance, if needed, and give information to the ambulance personnel.

First Aid Steps

CHECK the scene and the infant or child. Decide whether the area is safe for you to enter. Use disposable gloves if you think you might touch any body fluids or venom.

CALL the Poison Control Center at (800) 222-1222, or have someone else call, if possible.

CARE for the infant or child:

- Wash the bite area with soap and water.
- If the skin was broken, cover the area with a bandage.
- Keep the injured body part still and lower than the heart.
- Keep the infant or child calm and still.
- If the skin was broken or the infant or child is upset, call the parents or guardians and ask them to return home immediately.
- Provide care until the ambulance personnel or the parents or guardians arrive and take over.
- Fill out the Babysitter's Report Record (pages 40–42).
- Report to the parents or guardians when they arrive.

Bites, Spider

Note

- Don't try to catch the spider; remember what it looked like and describe it to the ambulance personnel and parents.

First Aid Steps

CHECK the scene and the infant or child. Decide whether the area is safe for you to enter. Use disposable gloves if you think you might touch any body fluids.

CALL 9-1-1 or the local emergency number, or have someone else call, if the infant or child has a reaction to the bite that involves:

- Trouble breathing;
- Uncontrollable coughing or wheezing; and
- Swelling of the face, neck or tongue.

CARE for the infant or child:

- Wash the bite area with soap and water.
- Apply a cold pack, such as ice in a plastic bag, to the bite. Place a thin cloth or towel between the skin and the cold pack.

◆ Call the parents or guardians and ask them to return home immediately.

◆ Provide care until the ambulance personnel or the parents or guardians arrive and take over.

◆ Fill out the Babysitter's Report Record (pages 40–42).

◆ Report to the parents or guardians when they arrive.

See also Allergic Reactions, page 120.

Bites, Tick

First Aid Steps

CHECK the scene and the infant or child. Decide whether the area is safe for you to enter. Use disposable gloves if you think you might touch any body fluids.

CARE for the infant or child:

- Using tweezers, grab the tick firmly and as close to the skin as possible. With a steady motion, pull the tick out slowly to avoid it breaking off in the skin.
- Place the tick in a sealed container — a jar or plastic refrigerator container (or tape it to a piece of paper).
- Wash the bite area with soap and water and use an antiseptic.

◆ Fill out the Babysitter's Report Record (pages 40–42). Note the location of the tick bite.

◆ Report to the parents or guardians when they arrive and give them the container with the tick.

Bites and Stings, Insect

Notes

- Bites and stings may be life threatening if the infant or child has an allergic reaction (see Allergic Reactions, page 120).
- Watch for signals of an allergic reaction and get help immediately if a reaction occurs.
- Find out in advance (see Family Interview Form) whether any children have any known allergic reactions to insect bites or stings. If so, find out what to do in case of a bite or sting.
- See also Bites, Tick, page 123; Bites, Spider, page 122.

First Aid Steps

CHECK the scene and the infant or child. Decide whether the area is safe for you to enter. Use disposable gloves if you think you might touch any body fluids.

CALL 9-1-1 or the local emergency number, or have someone else call, if the child has an allergic reaction or has trouble breathing (see Allergic Reactions, page 120).

CARE for the infant or child:

- Remove the stinger by scraping it away with a stiff object, such as a bank card or an identification card.
- Wash the area of the bite or sting with soap and water.
- Cover the area to keep it clean.
- Apply a cold pack, such as ice in a plastic bag, to the bite or sting. Place a cloth or towel between the skin and the cold pack.

◆ Call the parents or guardians if the infant or child:

- Looks or feels ill;
- Has an itchy rash that is spreading;
- Has nausea or vomiting; or
- Has trouble breathing.

◆ Provide care until the ambulance personnel or the parents or guardians arrive and take over.

◆ Fill out the Babysitter's Report Record (pages 40–42).

◆ Report to the parents or guardians when they arrive.

See also Allergic Reactions, page 120; Vomiting, page 148.

Bleeding

Note

- Serious bleeding can quickly become life threatening.

First Aid Steps

CHECK the scene and the infant or child. Decide whether the area is safe for you to enter. Use disposable gloves if you think you might touch any body fluids.

CALL 9-1-1 or the local emergency number, or have someone else call, if:

- Bleeding does not stop within a few minutes;
- Blood is spurting from the wound;
- The wound is on the stomach, the chest or there is a large wound to the hands or feet;
- You can see muscle or bone inside the wound;
- The wound is longer than 1 inch or looks deep;
- The wound has an object stuck in it (see Wounds, with Object, page 149); or
- Skin or body parts have been partially or completely torn away.

CARE for the infant or child:

- If there is a lot of bleeding, put a gauze pad or clean cloth over the wound and apply pressure.

- If the wound is on an arm or leg, lift the wounded part above the level of the heart, unless you think there are broken bones. Keep pressure on the wound.
- Cover the gauze pad with a roller bandage and continue to apply direct pressure over the wound.

- If blood soaks through, put more gauze pads and another roller bandage on top of the first bandage. Do not remove the first gauze pad and bandage; continue to keep pressure on the wound.

- If bleeding from arms or legs still does not stop, apply pressure at pressure points.
- During and after caring for bleeding, avoid touching other parts of your body such as your mouth, eyes or nose.

◆ Call the parents or guardians and ask them to return home immediately.

◆ Provide care until the ambulance personnel or the parents or guardians arrive and take over.

◆ Keep the infant or child from becoming cold or too warm.

◆ If there is minor bleeding:

- Put a clean gauze pad on the wound and apply pressure until the bleeding stops.
- Wash the area well with soap and water. Rinse well. Dry with a paper towel.
- Cover with an adhesive bandage.

◆ Fill out the Babysitter's Report Record (pages 40–42).

◆ "Report to the parents or guardians when they arrive.

Burns

Notes

- Burns can be caused by heat, chemicals (see Burns, Chemical, page 127), electricity and the sun.
- The area may appear red, brown, black or white; swell; and be painful.
- Do not touch an infant or child who is touching an electrical wire until you are ABSOLUTELY sure the power is turned off.

First Aid Steps

CHECK the scene and the infant or child. Decide whether the area is safe for you to enter. Use disposable gloves and cover the wound with a dressing as part of your care.

CALL 9-1-1 or the local emergency number, or have someone else call, for burns to the child or infant that:

- Cause trouble breathing;
- Cover more than one body part;
- Occur on the head, neck, hands, feet or genitals;
- Result from explosion or electricity; or
- Are deep (the skin has blisters or looks brown or black).

CARE for the infant or child:

- Remove the infant or child from the heat source.
- Cool the burn with water, unless it is an electrical burn (keep an electrical burn dry).
- Cover the burn with clean, dry dressings.
- Loosely bandage the dressing in place to prevent infection and reduce pain or cover the burned area with a dry sheet or towel.
- Keep the infant or child from becoming chilled or too warm.
- Help the infant or child rest comfortably.
- During and after caring for bleeding or burns, avoid touching other parts of your body such as your mouth, eyes or nose.
- ◆ For a severe burn, call 9-1-1, then the parents or guardians and ask them to return home immediately.
- ◆ Provide care until the ambulance personnel or parents or guardians arrive and take over.
- ◆ Fill out the Babysitter's Report Record (pages 40–42).
- ◆ Report to the parents or guardians when they arrive.

Burns, Chemical

Note
- Chemical burns should be flushed immediately with cool water.

First Aid Steps

CHECK the scene and the infant or child. Decide whether the area is safe for you to enter. Use disposable gloves if you think you might touch any body fluids or chemicals.

CALL the Poison Control Center at (800) 222-1222 after taking the steps listed under Care. If someone else is available, have him or her call the Poison Control Center while you begin care. Call 9-1-1, if advised to do so.

CARE for the infant or child:

- With a gloved hand, carefully brush powdered chemicals off the skin.
- Continuously flush chemical burns with cool water for 15-20 minutes or until the ambulance personnel arrive and take over.
  ○ For infants and young children, use the sink or shower, whichever is easier.
  ○ Older children can stand in the shower.
- Follow the Poison Control Center's further directions.
- Keep the infant or child from becoming chilled or too warm.
- Help the infant or child rest comfortably.

◆ For a severe burn, call 9-1-1, then the parents or guardians and ask them to return home immediately.

◆ Provide care until the ambulance personnel or parents or guardians arrive and take over.

◆ Fill out the Babysitter's Report Record (pages 40–42).

◆ Report to the parents or guardians when they arrive.

Checking a Conscious Infant or Child

First Aid Steps

CHECK the scene and the infant or child. Decide whether the area is safe for you to enter. Use disposable gloves if you think you might touch any body fluids. Check the child by asking these questions or, for the infant, by looking for answers to these questions:

- What happened?
- Are you having any trouble breathing?
- Are you in pain?
- Where are you hurt?
- Call out the infant's or child's name to check for a response.

Note: Don't ask the child to move body areas that hurt. Don't ask the child to move if you suspect an injury to the head, neck or back.

◆ Check toe to head:

- Before you begin, tell the child what you are going to do or talk in a soothing manner to an infant;

- Look over the body in general; and

- Look carefully for bleeding, cuts and bruises.

◆ Check the hips and legs (one leg at a time):

- Ask the child to:

- Move the toes, foot and ankle;

- Bend the leg; and

- For an infant, check for trembling or other movement of the legs.

◆ Check the arms:

- Check one arm at a time.

- Ask the child to:

- Move the hands and fingers;

- Bend the arm; and

- For an infant, check for trembling or other movement of the arms.

◆ Check the chest and stomach:

- Ask the child to take a deep breath and blow air out;

- Ask the child if there is any pain with breathing; and

- For an infant, watch for signs of discomfort when breathing.

◆ Check the shoulders:

- Ask the child to shrug his or her shoulders.

◆ Check the neck:

- Note any pain, discomfort or inability to move. If the child is not in pain and you do not suspect an injury to the head, neck or back, ask the child to move his or her head slowly from side to side.

- For an infant, watch for head movements.

◆ Check the head:

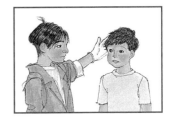

- Look at the scalp, face, ears, eyes, nose and mouth for cuts, bumps, bruises and depressions.

- Note if the infant or child is sleepy, not alert or confused.

◆ Check skin appearance and temperature:

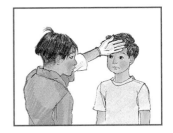

- Feel the infant's or child's forehead with the back of your hand.

- Look at the infant's or child's face and lips.

- Ask yourself, is the skin:

  ○ Cold or hot;

  ○ Unusually wet or dry;

  ○ Pale, bluish, ashen or flushed; or

  ○ Covered with hives or rash?

◆ If the infant or child can move all body parts without pain or discomfort and has no signals of life-threatening emergencies:

- Have him or her rest for a few minutes in a sitting position.

- Help the child SLOWLY stand when he or she is ready.

- Pick up and comfort the infant if there are no signals of an injury.

CALL 9-1-1 or the local emergency number, or have someone else call, if:

- The infant or child has a life-threatening emergency, such as not breathing.

- The infant or child cannot move a body part without pain (also call the parents or guardians after calling 9-1-1 or the local emergency number).

CARE for any conditions you find.

- ◆ Call the parents or guardians and explain the infant's or child's condition.
- ◆ Provide care until the ambulance personnel or the parents or guardians arrive and take over.
- ◆ Fill out the Babysitter's Report Record (pages 40–42).
- ◆ Report to the parents or guardians when they arrive.

Choking, Conscious Child

Notes

- A child who cannot speak, cough, cry or breathe might have a completely blocked airway due to choking and needs immediate care.
- A child who can cough only weakly or is making high-pitched sounds might have a partially blocked airway due to choking and needs immediate care.
- A child who is coughing forcefully may have an open air-way and may NOT need care unless the condition changes. Tell the child to continue coughing and watch the child closely to be sure the airway remains open.

First Aid Steps

CHECK the scene and the child. Decide whether the area is safe for you to enter. (Use disposable gloves if you think you might touch any body fluids.)

If the child cannot speak, cough, cry or breathe:

CALL If you are alone, provide care (as noted below) before calling 9-1-1 or the local emergency number.

CARE for the child:

- Stand or kneel behind the child, talk to the child and tell him or her what you are doing.
- Put the thumb side of your fist just above the child's belly button. Grasp your fist with your other hand.

- Give quick, upward thrusts until the object is coughed up or the child can speak, cough, cry or breathe or becomes unconscious.

- If the child becomes unconscious, lower him or her gently to the floor and place him or her on the side (in the recovery position; see Unconscious, Checking an Infant or Child, page 146) and call 9-1-1 if you have not already called. Return to the child when the dispatcher tells you to hang up.

- If the child can speak, cough, cry or breathe, help him or her rest comfortably, encourage coughing and watch to be sure he or she continues to be able to breathe.

◆ For any breathing emergency, call the parents or guardians and ask them to return home immediately.

◆ Provide care until the ambulance personnel or the parents or guardians arrive and take over.

◆ Fill out the Babysitter's Report Record (pages 40–42).

◆ Report to the parents or guardians when they arrive.

Choking, Conscious Infant

Notes

- An infant who cannot cough, cry or breathe might have a completely blocked airway due to choking and needs immediate care.

- An infant who can cough only weakly or is making high-pitched sounds might have a partially blocked airway due to choking and needs immediate care.

- An infant who is coughing forcefully may have an open airway and may NOT need care unless the condition changes. Watch the infant closely to be sure the airway remains open.

First Aid Steps

CHECK the scene and the infant. Decide whether the area is safe for you to enter. (Use disposable gloves if you think you might touch any body fluids.)

If the infant cannot cough, cry or breathe:

CALL If you are alone, provide care (as noted below) before calling 9-1-1 or the local emergency number.

CARE for the infant:

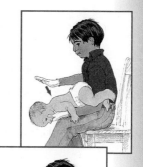

- Hold the infant face-down on your arm. Rest your arm on your thigh, with the infant's head lower than the body. Support the head with your fingers.

- With the heel of your other hand, strike the infant forcefully 5 times between the infant's shoulder blades.

- If the infant is still choking, support the infant between your arms and turn him or her face-up on your other thigh.

- Put 2 or 3 fingers on the center of the infant's breastbone, just below the nipples and give 5 chest thrusts, about 1 inch deep.

- Continue 5 back blows and 5 chest thrusts until the infant can cough, cry or breathe—or becomes unconscious.

  ○ If the infant becomes unconscious, lower him or her gently to the floor or carry the infant to the phone and call 9-1-1 or the local emergency number if you have not already called. Follow the 9-1-1 dispatcher's directions and continue to care for the infant by performing a head-tilt chin-lift (see Unconscious, Checking an Infant or Child, page 146). To learn what to do for an unconscious choking victim, you can enroll in an American Red Cross first aid or CPR class at your local Red Cross chapter.

◆ Call the parents or guardians and ask them to return home immediately.

◆ Provide care until the ambulance personnel or the parents or guardians arrive and take over.

◆ Fill out the Babysitter's Report Record (pages 40–42).

◆ Report to the parents or guardians when they arrive.

Cold Emergencies

Notes

- Hypothermia and frostbite are cold emergencies.
- Hypothermia is the general cooling of the body. The infant or child may be shivering or drowsy.
- Frostbite is the freezing of body parts. The skin looks waxy, flushed, white, gray, blue or black.

First Aid Steps

CHECK the scene and the infant or child. Decide whether the area is safe for you to enter. Use disposable gloves if you think you might touch any body fluids.

CALL 9-1-1 or the local emergency number, or have someone else call, if the infant or child:

- Has been exposed to the cold or feels cold to the touch and;
- Is unconscious;
- Is not breathing;
- Is very drowsy or sleepy when he or she should not be; or
- Has no feeling in a part of his or her body.

CARE for the infant or child:

- Gently move the infant or child to a warm place.
- If the infant or child is not breathing, give rescue breaths (see steps within Unconscious, Checking an Infant or Child, page 146) and make sure 9-1-1 or the local emergency number has been called after the first minute of care.
- Remove any wet clothing and dry the infant or child.
- Warm the infant or child slowly by wrapping him or her in blankets or by putting on dry clothing. You may place a hot water bottle wrapped in a towel or blanket next to the infant or child. Do not use an electric heating pad.
- Do not rub frostbitten parts. Soak in water (between 100-105°F). After rewarming, loosely bandage the affected area with dry, clean and sterile dressings.

- Call the parents or guardians and ask them to return home immediately.
- Provide care until the ambulance personnel or the parents or guardians arrive and take over.
- Fill out the Babysitter's Report Record (pages 40–42).
- Report to the parents or guardians when they arrive.

Ear Injury, Object in Ear

First Aid Steps

CHECK the scene and the infant or child. Decide whether the area is safe for you to enter. Use disposable gloves if you think you might touch any body fluid.

CALL 9-1-1 or the local emergency number, or have someone else call, if the infant or child is bleeding or if other fluid is draining from inside the child or infant's ear.

CARE for the infant or child:

- If there is an object in the ear or fluid draining from the ear, ask the child to turn his or her head to point the ear down or position an infant with the affected ear pointing down. The object may fall out or you may be able to gently pull the object from the ear with your fingers. Don't put any objects in the ear to try to remove the object.
- Pull down on the earlobe so that the object can fall out.
- Cover the ear lightly with a sterile dressing.
- Help the infant or child rest comfortably.
- If the infant or child has an insect in the ear, turn the head to point the ear up. The insect will often crawl out. It is frightening for a child to hear and feel an insect moving in the ear. Help the child remain calm.

- Call the parents or guardians if the object or insect does not come out. Explain the infant's or child's condition and ask them to return home immediately.
- Provide care until the ambulance personnel or the parents or guardians arrive and take over.
- Fill out the Babysitter's Report Record (pages 40–42).
- Report to the parents or guardians when they arrive.

Eye Injury, Object in Eye

Notes

- There may be injury around the eye and/or to the eyeball itself.
- Damage to the eyeball is very serious and can cause blindness.

First Aid Steps

CHECK the the scene and the infant or child. Decide whether the area is safe for you to enter. Use disposable gloves if you think you might touch any body fluids.

CALL 9-1-1 or the local emergency number, or have someone else call, if there is an object sticking out from the eye.

CARE for the infant or child:

- If there is an object sticking out of the eye:
  - Place the infant or child on his or her back;
  - Don't remove the object; and
  - Don't disturb an object in the eye. Hold the head still.

- If the child is old enough to understand, place something over the good eye so the child will not move the eyes looking around. If there is a chemical in the eye, pour a slow, steady stream of water over the eyeball from the nose outward, with the head leaning toward that side so water does not get in the "good" eye for 15-20 minutes. Call the Poison Control Center at (800) 222-1222 and go to the First Aid Action Plan for Burns, Chemical, page 127.

- If there is a small object, such as dirt, in the eye:
  - Have the child blink to try to flush the eye with tears.
  - Keep the child from rubbing the eye.
  - Gently flush the eye with cool water. Flush the eye from the nose outward.
  - If the object will not come out, close the eyelid and loosely cover the eye with a gauze pad.
  - Help the infant or child to rest comfortably.

- ◆ Call the parents or guardians if the object does not come out. Explain the infant's or child's condition and ask them to return home immediately.
- ◆ Provide care until the ambulance personnel or the parents or guardians arrive and take over.
- ◆ Fill out the Babysitter's Report Record (pages 40–42).
- ◆ Report to the parents or guardians when they arrive.

Head, Neck and Back Injuries

Notes

- If there is an injury to the head, there may also be injuries to the neck or back.
- Always look for a head, neck or back injury in these situations:
  - A hard object hit the top of the infant's or child's head;
  - The infant or child fell from a height greater than his or her own height;
  - The infant or child was found unconscious for unknown reasons;
  - An injury that has impacted the head or trunk;
  - An accident in which the child's helmet was cracked or broken; and
  - An incident involving a lightning strike.

First Aid Steps

CHECK the scene and the infant or child. Decide whether the area is safe for you to enter. Use disposable gloves if you think you might touch any body fluids.

CALL 9-1-1 or the local emergency number. If possible, have someone else call 9-1-1 and the parents or guardians while you provide care.

CARE for the infant or child:

- Place your hands on both sides of the infant's or child's head to keep it from moving.
- Check for breathing.
- If the child is not breathing, begin giving rescue breaths using the jaw-thrust maneuver (see steps within Unconscious, Checking an Infant or Child, page 146).

- Stop any bleeding (see Bleeding, page 125).
- Prevent the infant or child from becoming chilled or too warm.
- Keep the infant or child still and comfortable.
◆ If you are alone, call the parents or guardians as soon as the ambulance personnel arrive and take over.
◆ Provide care until the ambulance personnel or the parents or guardians arrive and take over.
◆ Fill out the Babysitter's Report Record (pages 40–42).
◆ Report to the parents or guardians when they arrive.

Heat Emergencies

Notes
- Heat emergencies are caused by overexposure to heat or being too active on a hot day.
- The infant or child may look or feel weak and tired, have a headache or feel dizzy.
- The skin may be hot, cool, moist or dry, depending on the infant or child's condition.

First Aid Steps

CHECK the scene and the infant or child. Decide whether the area is safe for you to enter. Use disposable gloves if you think you might touch any body fluids.

CALL 9-1-1 or the local emergency number, or have someone else call, if the infant or child has been in a warm place and:

- Feels dry and hot to the touch;
- Is dizzy or becomes unconscious;
- Begins to vomit; or
- Refuses water.

If you are alone, get the infant or child to a cool area, if possible, then call 9-1-1 and the parents or guardians. If someone else is available to call, have them call while you provide care.

CARE for the infant or child:

- Move the infant or child out of the heat immediately and to a cool place.

- Remove sweat-soaked clothing.
- If the infant or child feels hot and dry to the touch, apply cool, wet cloths.
- Fan the infant or child.
- If the infant or child is conscious and not nauseated, give him or her cool water to drink. (Lukewarm water is also good.)
- Help the infant or child to rest comfortably.

◆ Call the parents or guardians, explain the infant's or child's condition and ask them to return home immediately.
◆ Provide care until the ambulance personnel or the parents or guardians arrive and take over.
◆ Fill out the Babysitter's Report Record (pages 40–42).
◆ Report to the parents or guardians when they arrive.

Mouth Injuries

Note
- The mouth may be injured on the inside or outside. Injuries can affect the cheeks, tongue, lips or teeth.

First Aid Steps

CHECK the scene and the infant or child. Decide whether the area is safe for you to enter. Use disposable gloves if you think you might touch any body fluids.

CALL 9-1-1 or the local emergency number, or have someone else call, if the infant or child:

- Is not breathing;
- Has signals of a head, neck or back injury (see Head, Neck and Back Injuries, page 137);
- Becomes unconscious;
- Has trouble breathing; or
- Has bleeding that cannot be easily controlled.

CARE for the infant or child:

- If you don't suspect a serious head, neck or back injury:
  ○ Have the child lean slightly forward or place the infant or child on his or her side to prevent swallowing blood, which can cause nausea or vomiting.

139

- For bleeding inside the cheek:
  - Place a folded sterile dressing inside the mouth against the wound and apply pressure.
- For bleeding outside the cheek:
  - Put pressure directly on the wound with a sterile dressing.
- If an object is embedded in the cheek, go to the First Aid Action Plan for Wounds, with Object, page 149.
  - For a bleeding tongue or lips:

    Put direct pressure on the area with a sterile dressing. Once bleeding stops, let a child suck on a small piece of ice to relieve pain and reduce swelling.
- If a tooth has been knocked out:
  - Stop any bleeding by having the child bite down on a rolled sterile dressing put in the space left by the tooth;
  - Save any teeth by placing them in a container of milk, if possible, or water; and
  - Check for head, neck and back injuries (see Head, Neck and Back Injuries, page 137).

◆ For any serious injuries, call the parents or guardians and ask them to return home immediately. For a knocked out tooth, the child needs to go to the dentist very soon to save the tooth.

◆ Provide care until the ambulance personnel or the parents or guardians arrive and take over.

◆ Fill out the Babysitter's Report Record (pages 40–42).

◆ Report to the parents or guardians when they arrive.

Muscle, Bone and Joint Injuries

Notes
- You do not need to know what kind of injury it is to give first aid.

First Aid Steps

CHECK the infant or child. Decide whether the area is safe for you to enter. Use disposable gloves if you think you might touch any body fluids.

CALL 9-1-1 or the local emergency number, or have someone else call, for the following situations:

- The arm or leg is bent in an odd way;
- It feels or sounds like bones are rubbing together;
- You or the child heard a snap or pop when the injury happened;
- The infant or child cannot move or use the part normally;
- The injured area feels cold and numb;
- The injury involves the head, neck or back;
- The cause of the injury makes it seem really serious;
- There is a lot of swelling or a big bruise;
- You can see bone in the wound; and
- The injured infant or child has trouble breathing.

CARE for the infant or child:

- Do not move the injured part.
- Control any bleeding (see Bleeding, page 125).
- Apply a cold pack, such as ice in a plastic bag. Place a cloth or towel between the skin and the cold pack.

◆ Call the parents or guardians for any serious injuries and explain the infant's or child's condition and ask them to return home immediately.

◆ Provide care until the ambulance personnel or the parents or guardians arrive and take over.

◆ Fill out the Babysitter's Report Record (pages 40–42).

◆ Report to the parents or guardians when they arrive.

See also Bleeding, page 125.

Nosebleed

Notes

- A nosebleed is often caused by a blow to the nose.
- It also may be caused by an allergy, cold, nose picking or dry skin tissues.
- Bleeding is sometimes heavy at first.

First Aid Steps

CHECK the scene and the infant or child. Decide whether the area is safe for you to enter. Use disposable gloves if you think you might touch any body fluids.

CALL 9-1-1 or the local emergency number, or have someone else call, if bleeding cannot be controlled or if you suspect a head, neck or back injury (see Head, Neck and Back Injuries, page 137).

CARE for the infant or child:

- Have the child lean slightly forward, or sit up the infant and, while supporting, lean him or her slightly forward.
- You or the child should pinch the nostrils together for about 10 minutes.
- If the bleeding has not stopped after 10 minutes, apply a cold pack, such as ice in a plastic bag, to the bridge of the nose. Place a cloth or towel between the skin and the cold pack.
- If the bleeding still does not stop, put pressure on the upper lip just under the nose.
- When the bleeding stops, discourage the child from rubbing, blowing or picking his or her nose.

◆ If bleeding does not stop, call the parents or guardians, explain the infant's or child's condition and ask them to return home immediately.

◆ Provide care until the ambulance personnel or the parents or guardians arrive and take over.

◆ Fill out the Babysitter's Report Record (pages 40–42).

◆ Report to the parents or guardians when they arrive.

Poisoning

Notes

- Any substance is a poison if it causes injury or illness when it enters the body.
- A poison can get into the body by being swallowed, breathed in, touched or injected.
- Poisons can include household cleaners, medicines, plants, lawn chemicals, poison gases and even alcohol or tobacco.

- If you are unsure whether something a child or infant was exposed to is poisonous, call the Poison Control Center at (800) 222-1222.

First Aid Steps

CHECK the scene and the infant or child. Decide whether the area is safe for you to enter. If so, look for clues about what the infant or child might have eaten, drank or been exposed to. Use disposable gloves if you think you might touch any body fluids or the poison. Do not go into an area if it is unsafe.

CALL the Poison Control Center at (800) 222-1222 and bring the container of the poison to the phone. For any life-threatening condition (such as an unsafe scene, the child is unconscious, having trouble breathing or having seizures), call 9-1-1 or the local emergency number, or have someone else call if possible.

CARE for the infant or child:

- Move the infant or child away from the source of the poison.
- If the infant or child has trouble breathing or is not breathing, care for that life-threatening condition first (see Unconscious, Checking an Infant or Child, page 146). Then call 9-1-1 after 1 minute of care.
- Don't give the infant or child anything to eat or drink unless told to do so by the Poison Control Center or 9-1-1 dispatcher.
- Be ready to give the infant's or child's age and weight, allergies or medical conditions and his or her doctor's name and telephone number (this information should be listed on the Family Interview Form, pages 13–17).
- If the infant or child vomits, place the infant or child on his or her side and save what he or she threw up (see Vomiting, page 148).
- Follow the Poison Control Center's instructions.

◆ Call the parents or guardians, explain the infant's or child's condition and ask them to come home immediately.

◆ Provide care until the ambulance personnel or the parents or guardians arrive and take over.

◆ Fill out the Babysitter's Report Record (pages 40–42).

◆ Report to the parents or guardians when they arrive.

Seizures

Notes

- Some infants or children have seizure problems that their parents or guardians are aware of.
- Follow any specific instructions from parents or guardians on what to do if the infant or child has a seizure.

First Aid Steps

CHECK the scene and the infant or child. Decide whether the area is safe for you to enter. Use disposable gloves if you think you might touch any body fluids.

CALL 9-1-1 or the local emergency number, or have someone else call, if the seizure does not stop within 1 to 2 minutes; re-occurs; or if the child is injured, remains unconscious, is known to be diabetic, has a high fever, was poisoned or was electrocuted.

CARE for the infant or child:

- Remove any safety-related problems from around the infant or child during the seizure.
- Protect the infant's or child's head during the seizure by putting a thin cushion or a folded towel under it. Do not hold the infant or child down.
- Never force anything in the infant's or child's mouth.
- After the seizure, help the infant or child rest comfortably in a quiet place as the infant or child may be sleepy afterward.
- Check to see if the infant or child was injured during the seizure.
- Roll the infant or child onto his or her side to allow fluids, such as saliva, blood or vomit, to drain from the mouth.
- Help clean the infant or child if a toileting accident occurred during the seizure.

◆ Provide care until the ambulance personnel or the parents or guardians arrive and take over.

◆ Call the parents or guardians as soon as the ambulance personnel arrive and take over.

◆ Fill out the Babysitter's Report Record (pages 40–42).

◆ Report to the parents or guardians when they arrive.

Splinter

First Aid Steps

CHECK the scene and the infant or child. Decide whether the area is safe for you to enter. Use disposable gloves if you think you might touch any body fluids.

CARE for the infant or child:

- Soak the area with warm soapy water for about 10 to 15 minutes.
- Have the child sit where you have good light and the child can rest the affected body part on a firm surface. Secure an infant on the changing table and provide a toy for distraction, if possible.
- Using tweezers, grasp the splinter as close to the skin as possible and pull it out at the same angle it went in.
- Wash the wound again with soap and water.
- Cover the wound with an adhesive strip bandage.

- If you cannot remove the splinter:
  - ○ Wash the wound and cover it;
  - ○ Do not try to dig or cut the splinter out; and
  - ○ Wait for the parents or guardians to remove the splinter when they return home.

◆ Provide care until the parents or guardians arrive and take over.

◆ Fill out the Babysitter's Report Record (pages 40–42).

◆ Report to the parents or guardians when they arrive.

Stomachache

Notes

- A stomachache can be caused by many things, including spoiled food, overeating, constipation or stress.
- Sometimes young children (such as toddlers) do not recognize where discomfort comes from, so they call any discomfort a stomachache. The problem could be simply a need to go to the bathroom.

First Aid Steps

CHECK the scene and the infant or child. Decide whether the area is safe for you to enter. Use disposable gloves if you think you might touch any body fluids.

CALL the parents or guardians if the infant or child has a fever, difficulty producing urine (sometimes called "pee" or "number 1") or a long-lasting stomachache. Explain the infant or child's condition and ask the parents or guardians to return home.

◆ Call 9-1-1 or the local emergency number, or have someone else call, if the infant or child shows any life-threatening condition, or if the parents or guardians ask you to.

CARE for the infant or child:

● Help the infant or child rest comfortably and put a container nearby if the child needs to vomit.

◆ Provide care until the emergency medical personnel or the parents or guardians arrive and take over.

◆ Fill out the Babysitter's Report Record (pages 40–42).

◆ Report to the parents or guardians when they arrive.

See also Vomiting, page 148.

Unconscious, Checking an Infant or Child

Note

● Unconsciousness itself is a life-threatening condition.

First Aid Steps

CHECK the scene and the infant or child for responsiveness. Decide whether the area is safe. Use disposable gloves and breathing barriers if you think you might touch any body fluids.

● Tap the infant or child on the shoulder (and the foot on an infant) and shout to see if he or she responds.

If no response from the infant or child:

CALL 9-1-1 or the local emergency number. If you are alone and the child is under age 8, provide 1 minute of care before calling. Have someone else call, if possible. If you have to leave a child for any reason (e.g., calling 9-1-1 or letting EMS inside), put the child in a

recovery position. DO NOT put infants in a recovery position. They are not able to support themselves in this position. Instead, take the infant with you to call 9-1-1.

Continue checking:

○ If the infant or child is face-down, check breathing for 5 seconds without moving the infant or child; if the infant or child is not breathing or you cannot tell, gently turn the infant or child face-up and go to the next step.

○ With one hand on the forehead and two fingers under the tip of the chin, tilt the head back and lift the chin to open the airway (not as much for an infant). If you suspect a head, neck or back injury, you can use the jaw-thrust maneuver to open the airway.

○ Put your ear near the infant's or child's mouth. Look (at the chest), listen and feel for breathing for about 5 seconds.

If the infant or child is not breathing or you cannot tell:

• For an **infant**, keeping the head tilted slightly back and the chin lifted, take a breath and make a seal over the infant's nose and mouth with your mouth. Then:

○ Give 1 slow breath for about 1 1/2 seconds. Then take another breath and give 1 more slow breath.

• For a **child**, keeping the head tilted back and the chin lifted, pinch the nose shut, take a breath and make a seal over the child's mouth with your mouth. Then:

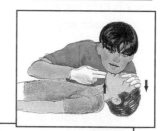

○ Give 1 slow breath for about 1 1/2 seconds. Then take another breath and give 1 more slow breath.

• Check the infant or child for signs of circulation (normal breathing, coughing or movement in response to rescue breaths) for **no more than 10 seconds.** Also check the infant or child from toe to head for severe bleeding.

CARE for the infant or child:

- Keep giving rescue breaths, 1 every 3 seconds until the infant or child starts breathing on his or her own, the scene becomes unsafe, you are too tired to continue or ambulance personnel arrive and take over.
- Recheck for signs of circulation and breathing after the first minute and then every minute after that.

If the infant or child vomits and you do not suspect a head, neck or back injury, roll him or her onto the side to keep the airway open and allow fluids to drain from the mouth.

- ◆ If you are alone, call the parents or guardians as soon as the ambulance personnel arrive and take over and ask them to return home immediately.
- ◆ Provide care until the ambulance personnel or the parents or guardians arrive and take over.
- ◆ Fill out the Babysitter's Report Record (pages 40–42).
- ◆ Report to the parents or guardians when they arrive.

Vomiting

Note

- Dehydration can occur quickly with infants and children and therefore fluids need to be replaced.

First Aid Steps

CHECK the scene and the infant or child. Decide whether the area is safe for you to enter. Use disposable gloves if you think you might touch any body fluids.

CALL 9-1-1 or the local emergency number, or have someone else call, if the infant or child vomits blood or is unconscious.

CARE for the infant or child:

- Put a bowl or basin nearby in case the child needs to vomit more.
- Clean the infant or child. Help the child rinse his or her mouth and blow his or her nose, as needed.
- Let the child sip water every 5 minutes for 30 to 60 minutes. For an infant, offer a bottle with room temperature water.
- Help the infant or child rest comfortably.
- If the infant or child has vomited and becomes unconscious but is still breathing, roll him or her onto the side to allow the vomit to drain from the mouth. Keep an infant from lying on his or her stomach.

- Call the parents or guardians if the infant or child vomits more than once. Explain the infant's or child's condition. Ask the parents or guardians to come home.
- Provide care until the ambulance personnel or the parents or guardians arrive and take over.
- Fill out the Babysitter's Report Record (pages 40–42).
- Report to the parents or guardians when they arrive.

See also Stomachache, page 145.

Wounds, with Object

Notes

- A wound with an object stuck in it will be more difficult to care for than other wounds.
- Do not remove an object, such as a nail, large piece of glass or knife, since it could cause more bleeding and further harm.

First Aid Steps

CHECK the scene and the infant or child. Decide whether the area is safe for you to enter. Use disposable gloves if you think you might touch any body fluids.

CALL 9-1-1 or the local emergency number, or have someone else call, if possible.

CARE for the infant or child:

- Do not remove the object (except for dirt or a splinter; see Splinter, page 145).
- Place bulky dressings (rolls of gauze, clean socks or other clean cloth) around the object to hold it in place.
- Bandage the dressing and object in place so the object does not move.
- Control the bleeding (see Bleeding, page 125).

- Call the parents or guardians, explain the infant's or child's condition and ask them to come home immediately.
- Provide care until the ambulance personnel or the parents or guardians arrive and take over.
- Fill out the Babysitter's Report Record (pages 40–42).
- Report to the parents or guardians when they arrive.

GLOSSARY

Accident: Any unexpected or unplanned event that may result in injury, death or a combination of serious effects.

Airway: The pathway through which air moves from the mouth and nose to the lungs.

Allergic Reaction: A negative reaction of the body to certain insect stings, foods or medications.

Ammunition: Bullets or explosive materials used in guns.

Ashen: Absence of color or grayish color; darker skin often looks ashen instead of pale.

Asthma: A condition that narrows the air passages and causes trouble breathing.

Avulsions: An injury where the skin or body parts have been partially or completely torn away.

Bite: An injury to the skin caused by an insect, animal or human.

Body Fluids: Liquid substances produced by the body, including urine, saliva and blood.

Breathing Barriers: A protective breathing device used when giving rescue breaths that can prevent contact with blood or other body fluids. Face shields and masks are types of breathing barriers.

Check-Call-Care: Three emergency action steps you take in an emergency.

Child Abuse: The physical, psychological or sexual assault on a child, resulting in injury or emotional trauma.

Choking: A life-threatening emergency where the airway is partially or completely blocked. If the airway is completely blocked, an infant or child cannot cough, speak, cry or breathe.

Cold Pack: A waterproof package containing ice or other frozen solids used in first aid to prevent or reduce swelling.

Conscious: When a person is awake or has not fainted.

Constipation: The inability to have a bowel movement.

Corrective Feedback: Identifying an error and giving the correction in a nonjudgmental and positive manner.

Croup: A type of infection of the breathing tract that occurs in infants and small children.

Cut: A break in the skin's surface.

Dehydration: When a person loses a lot of water (or body fluids) from their body without replacing it.

Developmental Stages: The stages a person goes through from birth to old age; each stage involves physical, mental, emotional and social changes.

Discipline: Actions taken to guide a child to better behavior.

Dispatcher: Emergency phone operator who can send medical, police or fire personnel to assist with an emergency.

Disposable Gloves: Thin, waterproof gloves worn to keep germs off of the hands when contacting any body fluid, such as blood or vomit. Available in latex, nitrile or vinyl.

Diversity: The differences found among people and their lifestyles.

Drowning: Death by suffocating in water.

Emergency: A problem situation where action is needed right away because someone is injured or ill.

Environment: Surrounding or condition.

Feces: Solid body waste. Sometimes called "bowel movements," "poop," or "number 2."

First Aid: Care given to someone who is hurt or sick until more advanced care can be obtained. When provided in the first few minutes of an emergency, it can save a life.

First Aid Action Plan: A plan that explains how to respond to different kinds of injuries and illnesses.

Flammable: Something that can easily catch on fire.

Formula: A milk-based or soybean-based liquid mixture given to infants using a bottle.

Germs: Tiny living organisms that cannot be seen by the human eye. Some germs cause infection and disease; others are harmless and some are even useful.

Hygiene: Activities like brushing your teeth or washing your hair and hands that help keep your body clean and healthy.

Infant: A baby younger than 12 months old.

Infectious: Able to cause disease.

Leadership: Acting responsibly and taking charge of a situation.

Minor Bleeding: Bleeding that usually stops by itself within a few minutes.

Nausea: The feeling that can occur before vomiting. Feeling sick to the stomach.

Pale: Absence of color. To lose color, to appear ashen or white.

Poison Control Center: A special health care center that gives information to the public in cases of poisoning or suspected poisoning emergencies. The national number is (800) 222-1222.

Poisoning: Eating, drinking, breathing or injecting a solid, liquid or gas that can injure or even kill you when taken into the body or put on the surface of the skin.

Positive Feedback: An acknowledgement of correct behavior.

Preschooler: A child 3 to 5 years old.

Puncture Wound: An injury to the skin caused by piercing with a pointed object.

Recovery Position: Lying on one side with the face angled toward the ground to protect and maintain an open airway for an unconscious child who is breathing and does not have a head, neck or back injury.

Rescue Breaths: A method of breathing for someone who cannot.

Résumé: A list of one's experience, skills and abilities for performing a job.

Role Model: Someone who acts in a responsible way for others to imitate.

Rubber Pants: Waterproof garment placed over an infant's diaper to prevent leakage of body wastes.

Safety Covers: Plastic protective covers put into or over an unused electrical outlet to prevent children from being shocked or burned.

Safety Gate: A low, often removable, gate to keep infants and toddlers away from stairs or other dangerous areas.

Safety Rails or Sides: The bars or slats on the side of a crib or bed that prevent an infant or child from falling out.

School-Aged Child: A child 5 years and older.

Scrape: A wound where the skin has been rubbed away.

Security Bars: Window or door bars that protect a home from intruders and are locked from the inside.

Seizure: Trembling, shaking or falling to the ground because of disturbed electrical output in the brain. This can be caused by an ongoing health problem, poisoning, a high fever or head injury.

Severe Bleeding: Bleeding that squirts from the wound or cannot be stopped easily.

Signs of Circulation: Signs that show that a victim's heart is beating. These include normal breathing and coughing or movement in response to rescue breaths.

Sterile: Free from germs.

Strangled: A blocked airway; cutting off someone's breathing.

Suffocate: Not being able to breathe. The absence of breathing.

Toddler: A child 1 to 3 years old.

Toileting: Urinating or having a bowel movement into a toilet. A child usually is toilet trained between 2 to 5 years of age.

Unconscious: When a person is not awake or has fainted. The person is not aware of his or her surroundings.

Urine: Liquid body waste while going to the bathroom. Often called different terms such as "pee" or "number 1."

Vomit: To throw up what is in the stomach through the mouth.

Wheezing: A hoarse, whistling sound during breathing that usually signals a breathing problem.

Wound: An injury to the body.

INDEX

REFERENCES

● ● ●

American Academy of Pediatric Dentistry. Available at http://www.aapd.org. Accessed on July 29, 2002.

American Heart Association. 2000 Guidelines for Cardiopulmonary Resuscitation and Emergency Cardiovascular Care. *Circulation*;102(8): August 22, 2000.

American Heart Association. *2002 Heart and Stroke Statistical Update*. Dallas, TX: American Heart Association, 2000.

American Red Cross. *Community First Aid and Safety*. Washington, DC: StayWell, 2002.

American Red Cross. *First Aid Fast*. Washington, DC: StayWell, 2002.

American Red Cross. *First Aid for Children Today*. Washington, DC: StayWell, 1992.

Centers for Disease Control and Prevention. Facts About Lyme Disease. Available at http://www.cdc.gov/od/oc/media/fact/lyme.htm. Accessed on February 7, 2001.

Epilepsy Foundation of America. Epilepsy: A Report to the Nation. Available at http://www.efa.org/epusa/nation/nation.html. Accessed on February 26, 2001.

Epilepsy Foundation of America. Seizure Recognition and First Aid Brochure, 2000.

Jeffery HE, Megevand A, Page HD as quoted by Sudden Infant Death Syndrome Network. Available at http://www.sids-network.org/experts/prone-risk.html. Accessed on February 7, 2001.

Litovitz TL, Klein-Schwartz W, Caravati EM, Youniss J, Crouch B, Lee S. 1998 Annual Report of the American Association of Poison Control Centers Toxic Exposure Surveillance System. *Amer J Emer Med* 1999;17(5):435-87.

National Center for Injury Prevention and Control, Centers for Disease Control and Prevention. Scientific Data, Surveillance, & Injury Statistics. Available at http://www.cdc.gov/ncipc/osp.data.htm. Accessed on February 12-14, 2001.

National Fire Protection Association. NFPA Fact Sheet on Home Fire Statistics. Available at http://www.nfpa.org. Accessed on February 20, 2001.

National Heart, Lung and Blood Institute, National Institutes of Health. 2000. Available at http://www.nhlbi.nih.gov. Accessed on February 12, 2001.

National Maternal Child Health Clearinghouse. Available at http://www.nmchc.org. Accessed on January 30, 2001.

National Safe KIDS Campaign. Available at http://www.safekids.org. Accessed on March 20, 2001.

Palm Beach Herpetological Society in Cooperation with the Florida Cooperative Extension Service, Institute of Food and Agricultural Sciences, University of Florida. Venomous Snake Bite. Available at http://www.cdc.gov.niosh/nasd/docs/as31600.html. Accessed on February 20, 2001.

Students Against Destructive Decisions. Available at www.saddonline.com. Accessed on March 30, 2001.

Sudden Infant Death Syndrome Alliance. Facts About Sudden Infant Death Syndrome. Available at http://www.sidsalliance.org. Accessed on February 7, 2001.

US Consumer Product Safety Commission. Available at http://www.cpsc.gov. Accessed on January 30, 2001.

For information about these supporting organizations, please visit their Web sites

Boy Scouts of America
www.bsa.scouting.org

Boys & Girls Clubs of America
www.bgca.org

Consumer Product Safety Commission
www.cpsc.gov

4-H
www.national4-hheadquarters.gov

Girl Scouts of the USA
www.girlscouts.org

JCC Association
www.jcca.org

YMCA
www.ymca.net

ANSWER KEY TO ACTIVITIES
● ● ●

Shining Star Game:

1. responsible
2. communicates
3. professional
4. business practices

Factoid Challenge:

"Factoids": 3, 5, 9, 10, 11, 12
Decoys: 1, 2, 4, 6, 7, 8, 13

Toy Box Jumble:

see next page →

First Aid Puzzle:

Answers:

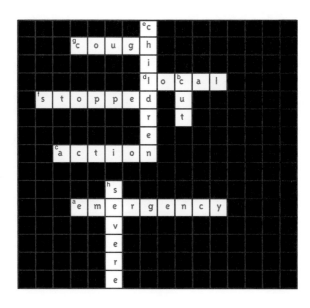

Answers:

E	E	H	H	S	T	N	I	A	P	R	E	G	N	I	F	G	A	B	O
A	A	Z	R	S	S	T	T	Y	L	E	P	P	Q	B	N	M	M	T	B
N	R	R	C	A	N	A	R	C	T	R	I	C	Y	C	L	E	O	H	E
T	J	A	T	T	U	V	H	O	P	G	H	B	E	E	T	J	O	L	N
K	S	T	E	E	T	H	I	N	G	R	I	N	G	B	B	G	C	R	T
L	A	T	D	E	M	C	C	R	S	R	G	B	J	O	D	D	T	D	B
B	I	L	D	N	A	H	H	S	N	T	C	I	I	O	O	S	E	A	D
C	J	E	S	S	E	S	O	O	G	K	C	U	D	K	C	U	D	V	E
S	R	H	E	C	L	H	P	Q	Q	E	I	Q	R	S	E	S	S	V	L
Q	P	H	K	O	O	L	K	L	L	H	O	G	Q	D	A	A	B	S	I
C	K	E	O	B	S	T	A	C	K	I	N	G	R	I	N	G	S	N	B
T	R	P	C	L	H	K	Z	B	Y	Z	M	N	O	P	N	S	S	T	O
S	T	C	C	N	M	J	K	U	T	C	A	F	F	P	K	E	D	K	M
L	Y	E	D	M	D	R	A	O	B	E	T	A	K	S	F	F	O	A	L
R	L	P	E	E	K	A	B	O	O	C	K	O	G	F	F	O	N	M	L
J	E	P	T	M	H	N	F	F	P	C	W	S	M	M	B	I	P	V	K
O	F	G	O	M	E	L	F	G	B	D	W	U	A	T	T	I	Q	J	V
H	C	O	M	M	L	E	A	A	B	N	X	N	S	B	R	A	L	A	K
N	Q	S	P	J	M	S	S	T	O	R	B	O	T	U	P	A	N	K	A

teething ring
stacking ring
mobile
rattle
peek-a-boo
books

Toys

tricycle
finger paints
mobile
books

Toys

tricycle
finger paints
Duck Duck Goose
mobile
books

Toys

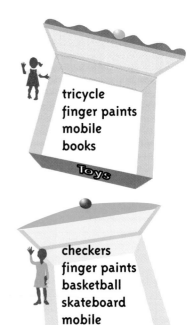

checkers
finger paints
basketball
skateboard
mobile
books

Toys

Family Information Cards

Child's Name: 　Age (Birthday): 　Weight:	**Parent or Guardian Name:** **Parent or Guardian Name:**
Address:	**Nearest Cross Street:**
Phone Number Where **Parent or Guardian Will Be:**	**Phone Number:**
Neighbor's Name: **Neighbor's Phone Number:**	**Cell or Pager Phone Number:**
Doctor's Name: **Doctor's Phone Number:**	**Local Emergency** **Phone Number:**
Poison Control Center: **(800) 222-1222**	**Evacuation Location:** **Emergency Contact:**

Child's Name: 　Age (Birthday): 　Weight:	**Parent or Guardian Name:** **Parent or Guardian Name:**
Address:	**Nearest Cross Street:**
Phone Number Where **Parent or Guardian Will Be:**	**Phone Number:**
Neighbor's Name: **Neighbor's Phone Number:**	**Cell or Pager Phone Number:**
Doctor's Name: **Doctor's Phone Number:**	**Local Emergency** **Phone Number:**
Poison Control Center: **(800) 222-1222**	**Evacuation Location:** **Emergency Contact:**

MISSION OF THE AMERICAN RED CROSS

The American Red Cross, a humanitarian organization led by volunteers and guided by its Congressional Charter and the Fundamental Principles of the International Red Cross Movement, will provide relief to victims of disaster and help people prevent, prepare for, and respond to emergencies.

ABOUT THE AMERICAN RED CROSS

The American Red Cross is dedicated to helping make families, schools and communities safer at home and around the world.

A humanitarian service organization, the American Red Cross annually mobilizes relief to the victims of more than 63,000 disasters nationwide and has been the primary supplier of lifesaving blood and blood products in the United States for more than 50 years. The American Red Cross also trains more than 11.7 million people in vital lifesaving skills, provides direct health services to 2.5 million people, provides more than 24 million locally relevant community services, assists international disaster and conflict victims in more than 50 countries, and transmits nearly 1.4 million emergency messages between members of the U.S. Armed Forces and their families.

FUNDAMENTAL PRINCIPLES OF THE INTERNATIONAL RED CROSS AND RED CRESCENT MOVEMENT

HUMANITY

IMPARTIALITY

NEUTRALITY

INDEPENDENCE

VOLUNTARY SERVICE

UNITY

UNIVERSALITY